GREY PAES AND BACON

A JOURNEY TO THE HEART OF THE BLACK COUNTRY

Bob Bibby

Edited by Joss Guttery
Published by TravellersEye

Grey Paes And Bacon

1st Edition

Published by TravellersEye Ltd 2001

Head Office:

Colemore Farm

Colemore Green

Bridgnorth

Shropshire

WV16 4ST

United Kingdom

tel: (0044) 1746 766447   fax: (0044) 1746 766665

email: books@travellerseye.com   website: www.travellerseye.com

Set in Times

ISBN: 1903070066

Printed and bound in Great Britain by Creative Print & Design.

Map extracts reproduced from GEO projects' Birmingham Canal Navigations map with permission of the publisher Geoprojects (UK) Ltd. tel: 0118 9393567

e-mail enquiries@geoprojects.demon.co.uk

To my Black Country friends, in the hope that they approve.

Special thanks to the following:

Steve Bull & Rachel Heyhoe-Flint of Wolverhampton
Wanderers F.C.,
Mike Cooper of Avery Berkel, Councillor Lord Tarsem
King, Roy McCauley & Nigel Haynes of Sandwell
M.B.C., Councillor Tim Sunter of Dudley M.B.C.,
Warren Wilson and Rob Davies of the *Express & Star,*
Ajit Sahota, Ron Watson, Roy Boffy and Steve Clarke.

Very special thanks to Enid and Sue, for sparing us for a
few days.

Extraspecial thanks to John Gorman, my companion and
friend.

Whan that Aprill with his shoures soote
The droghte of March hath perced to the roote
Than longen folk to goon on pilgrimages.

Geoffrey Chaucer: Prologue to The Canterbury Tales

The Black Country, black by day and red by night, cannot be matched, for vast and varied production, by any other space of equal radius on the surface of the globe.

Elihu Burritt: Walks in the Black Country

By any standards they were the biggest mass murderers the Black Country has ever known. The percentage of Black Country miners killed who worked in the Earls of Dudley's pits varied from 10% in the 1850s and 60s to more than 20% in the 1890s.

George J. Barnsby: Social Conditions in the Black Country 1800-1900

Cum on feel the noize.

Slade

About The Author

Bob Bibby was brought up and went to school in Wolverhampton. After university, he taught English in schools in Rowley Regis and Dudley. He then became a school inspector, working in the Black Country and further afield, and later a part-time teacher at the University of Birmingham. In recent years he has moved to live in south Shropshire, where he devotes most of his time to writing. He is married and has two grown-up daughters.

At various times he has been a bus conductor, a scout leader, a folk singer, a football team manager, a pea packer, a parish councillor, a hot dog salesman, a cross-country runner, a skiffle group leader, a crossword compiler and chair of a national association.

His first crime novel in the Tallyforth Mystery series, entitled *Be a Falling Leaf*, was published in 1998 and the second, *Bird on the Wing*, in 2000. The third in the series, entitled *The Liquidator* and based in Wolverhampton, is likely to appear some time in 2001.

Grey Paes and Bacon is his first travel book.

The Route

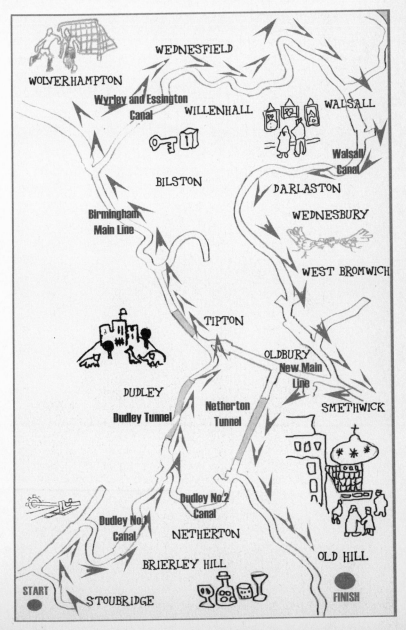

WOLVERHAMPTON

WEDNESFIELD

Wyrley and Essington Canal

WILLENHALL

WALSALL

Walsall Canal

BILSTON

DARLASTON

WEDNESBURY

Birmingham Main Line

WEST BROMWICH

TIPTON

OLDBURY New Main Line

SMETHWICK

DUDLEY

Dudley Tunnel

Netherton Tunnel

Dudley No.1 Canal

Dudley No.2 Canal

NETHERTON

OLD HILL

BRIERLEY HILL

START

STOUBRIDGE

FINISH

FOREWORD

When Bob asked me if I would like to join him on a walk along some of the Black Country's canal banks, I wasn't sure what my role was to be: observer, companion or minder.

I had, of course, heard of the Black Country, but it could have been darkest Africa for all my knowledge of it. I have caught many a train from Wolverhampton to London, and I now realise that they have crawled through that very 'Country', and I have flirted with its environs when driving the back way from Birmingham to Bridgnorth.

Amongst my many pleasures is a love of walking and of being near water (I won't go into some of the rest, certainly not in this sort of book). Here was an opportunity not only to satisfy my appetites but also to penetrate the interior of this 'little-known continent' on a walk of discovery, which it truly was; every step taking me to places whose names were, to me, as strange as Timbuktu's.

I have a vibrant love of life and people, and, by braving the elements and the Black Country accent, I was able to see an area rich in history, industry and character.

Since the walk, I have sung the praises of the canals to one and all, and I am sure that any reader who decides to emulate the two tepid (sic) walkers, who walked for five days to make this book possible, will break into similar song.

Have a nice walk.

John Gorman
Bridgnorth, 2001

INTRODUCTION

ON A PERSONAL NOTE

I come from the Black Country.

For a long time, I have been slightly embarrassed to say that.

You need to know at the start that I never meant to come from the Black Country. Given the choice, I'd have been the son of the British Ambassador to China, then a teenage runaway to the French Foreign Legion, and then a deserter starving in an attic on the Left Bank in Paris writing my first great novel, whose fantastic worldwide success would take me to a life of wine, women and song in California, with possibly a starring role in a Hollywood biopic en route.

Of course, none of that ever happened. Blame my parents, if you like, though it was hardly their fault that the child they produced was not the offspring of some brilliant scholar with a fluency in Mandarin language and a deep understanding of Ming politics but the child of a secretary and an optician. It was the latter who was responsible for me living in the Black Country, because that was where my dad got his first job shortly before the outbreak of the Second World War. My dad was a Lancastrian and my mum a Scot, so it is quite possible that my family's time in the Black Country might have been brief but, in September of 1939, Adolf Hitler and Neville Chamberlain changed all that. Even then, the likelihood that I would spend all my life in the Black Country might have been avoided because, when my dad was called up into the army, my mum returned to stay with her parents and my grandparents-to-be in Aberdeen in north-east Scotland.

And that's where I was conceived, nurtured and eventually born.

Who knows where I might have ended up had history turned out differently? My dad might have been killed in battle and I might have remained in Aberdeen, ending up perhaps as Rector of Aberdeen University or, more likely, as an out-of-work fisherman. Or he might have been captured by the Germans and imprisoned in Colditz, where he could have met Richard Attenborough (or was it Jack Hawkins?) and helped to dig the tunnel that allowed hundreds of brave British squaddies to escape through Germany with passports made from baked toilet paper, a smattering of useful German phrases such as "Gott in Himmel!" and "Hand i hoch!", and greatcoats made from blankets stained with tea. On the other hand, Hitler might have decided not to invade Russia, the Third Reich might have established itself for a thousand years in Britain, and I might have ended up as a pen-pusher in Brussels, drafting laws designed to create a German-dominated United States of Europe!

But that's just a silly fantasy.

As it turned out, the war ended, my dad was demobbed and the family returned to live in Wolverhampton. I was four years old and I have no recall of this event that was to be one of the most momentous in my life - my glorious entry into the cauldron of the universe, where I was to learn, unwittingly, to speak a language that Geoffrey Chaucer would probably have recognised and where I was to spend virtually the whole of the remainder of my life.

According to my mum, I was late in talking and my first words were uttered in the Black Country. When questioned as to why I hadn't spoken before, I apparently replied:

'Hitherto there has been nothing worth remarking upon.'

Actually I've pinched that story. It was the historian Thomas Carlyle who reputedly behaved in this manner and I don't think it was quite like that with me. But, whatever the truth, I came to live in the Black Country, I began my schooling in the Black Country, I became a conscious person in the Black Country. In short, I found my voice in the Black Country.

My young life was circumscribed by the Wolverhampton area. I don't believe we had a car until I was nine or ten, so we didn't travel much. True, I had a bicycle but, when my mates and I went out biking, it was into the Staffordshire countryside around Kinver, not into the industrialised areas, that we pedalled. So I knew little about most of the Black Country apart from the names of its towns and the black smoky pall that hung over it when I looked south from the top of Sedgley Beacon.

I doubt if my young life was essentially very different from that of most English youngsters, then or now. Unless you're incredibly lucky, incredibly observant, and incredibly unaware of the all-pervasive effects of your sexual growth, you just don't take in much of what's around you geographically when you're young, except insofar as it affects you directly. You know about the hills you have to climb, by foot or by bike, because they knacker you (unless you're pretending to yourself that you're actually Alf Tupper or Wilson from *The Wizard*). You know the shortest way from A to B, because you sometimes have to do it when it's teeming down with rain. You know where X is, because you have to go to school there. You know where Y is, because that's where your dentist is. And you know where Z is, because that's where Jill or John lives and your life won't be complete until you see them again and seek "a consummation devoutly to be wished".

So the furthest I got into the Black Country as a youngster was in my teens, when I belonged to a skiffle group. Virtually everybody did at the time. This collective madness took hold of the young males of the United Kingdom which led them to believe that, if they could gather together a washboard, a tea chest with a piece of string, and a home-made guitar, then learn the challenging lyrics to *It Takes a Worried Man* or *Pick a Bale of Cotton*, they were on the way to becoming musical superstars. And, as everybody knows, some of them did just that. I've often thought that, if Wolverhampton had been Liverpool, I might have been Paul McCartney. On the other hand, knowing my luck I might have been John Lennon and dead!

Anyway, our skiffle group was called The Livewires. Don't ask me why, because I can't remember. Somebody must have dreamed it up and thought it was cool. And that somebody would have been either Mick who played the brown-painted tea chest bass, Fob who played his mum's washboard, Miles with the home-made guitar, whose real name was Dave but who was training to be a ladies' hairdresser, or me who was what they now call lead vocalist and guitarist. I also can't remember why I was the lead singer but I suspect it was because it was my garage that we practised in.

Only fair, eh?

We only made two public appearances, both in Bilston. The first was at the Saturday morning matinee at what was then The Palace cinema. We had no amplification but thought that, if we shouted, that would be good enough. Of course, it wasn't. We were crap. And we got a load of crap thrown at us by the assembled trainee Bilston criminals - peanuts, sweet wrappers, dead chewing gum, and so forth. Our second showing was at the Bilston Carnival in Hickman Park in a skiffle competition in which we came fourth out of five. We would have come fifth but one group was disqualified for having an amplifier.

I have tried to escape, believe me. My first real attempt was at eighteen when I went away to university. This should have provided a natural end to my days in the Black Country. I was well prepared, having had my Black Country accent and dialect surgically removed by The Grammar School and replaced with a particularly useful knowledge of Greek and Latin verbs. This remarkable educational strategy has proved successful with others, who have gone on to become captains of the civil service or renowned scholars at Oxford or Cambridge. Sadly, with me it failed because the most important things I learned at university were concerned with shove ha'penny, Newcastle Brown Ale, horse-racing and sex. My plan at the end of my time at university was to travel to Greece and live on a boat while I wrote poetry.

Of course, I didn't. Instead I came home, armed with my degree, and went off on my Vespa scooter to work in Rowley Regis. Thus began my second introduction to the Black Country, seen through the eyes and heard through the voices of the mini-skirted Blackheath and Rowley wenches and their Levi-jeaned chaps.

After three years I tried to escape again. There was at the time a scheme in the job I was doing for a year's training in order to achieve a further qualification. So I applied and was granted this one year's training, which by good chance coincided with a pal of mine being given a year off by his Canadian university to continue his studies in London. And that was where, would you believe, my course was too. Well, you can guess, can't you? We both had plans to publish our first novels and head up the next generation of leading young British writers.

You know what happened, of course. That's right, I came back to the Black Country and within twelve months had moved to a new job in Netherton. There I discovered Ma Pardoe's delicious beer, Cradley Heathens speedway and the canal towpaths of the Black Country. At the same time I started, with a group of mates, running a folk club at the Old Mill in Sedgley. I was part of the resident singing group. And you'll never guess what we were called - yes, with stunning originality, The Millers!

From Netherton I moved to Kingswinford, where I worked for a further ten years. The birth of my children and a very full working life gave me little time or desire for further geographical exploration and it was only when I was appointed to a consultancy post in Dudley that I began to refamiliarise myself with certain parts of the Black Country, like Sedgley, the Gornals, Stourbridge and Dudley itself, and to get to know properly for the first time other parts, such as Halesowen, Cradley, Coseley and Brierley Hill. Only then did I really begin to feel I was developing an understanding of the area which life had chosen for me to inhabit, even though I'd been living in it for the best part of thirty-five years already.

Thoughts of escape had long gone, together with all the other romantic nonsenses of youth. Besides, I had come to love my Black Country. When someone on holiday in Majorca told me that I spoke like a Brummie, I took terrific pleasure in telling them to "goo ter Brierley Hill" and why! And when my younger daughter a few years later returned from her first term at university in Leeds to tell that she had been called a "yam yam" because she came from the Black Country, I was ready to ask the name-caller outside in order to defend its honour.

In recent years, my work has taken me into parts of Walsall, which I knew little of at one time, and into parts of what is now known as Sandwell, while my links with Wolverhampton and Dudley have, for a variety of reasons connected with friends and family, remained as strong as ever. However, it has been in travelling across the area in these years and in seeing the huge changes that have occurred within it that I have gradually developed a desire to record the modern flavour of what is known as the Black Country.

So, this is a personal odyssey through the Black Country, where I have lived, worked and played for over half a century. Though I have included some historical information, I have not attempted to write the definitive history of the places I visit; others have done that already and better than I could. Nor have I tried to include every town and village in the Black Country, tempting though it was. Instead I chose to follow a particular route through the area and that route has been the determiner of what I write about. This means that some places, such as Sedgley and Lye for instance, are barely mentioned. That's a little unfortunate but so is life!

My purpose is to describe the individual flavours of the area which Thomas Carlyle, the late historian, described in 1824 as "a frightful scene" and which the American consul in Birmingham in 1868 described as "black by day and red by night" but which the modern day Black Country Museum was set up "to preserve and to communicate to the widest possible audience".

To find out why was the purpose of my journey.

ONE

THE BLACK COUNTRY

So, you're asking, if you're not already living there, where is the Black Country? What is the Black Country? And why should anyone give a flying kipper about it?

Well, I'll tell you.

First and most important, the Black Country does NOT include Birmingham. It is that part of the West Midlands to the west of England's second largest city, which broadly encompasses the present-day boroughs of Dudley, Sandwell, Walsall, and Wolverhampton. Originally - and if you're a real Black Country-anorak, you'd be sniffily insistent upon this - it was a term used to describe the geographical area stretching from south Staffordshire to the borders of Birmingham, straddling the ridge of hills running south-east from Wolverhampton. Beneath this area lay the "Staffordshire Thirty Foot Coal Seam" which, curiously enough, averaged thirty feet in thickness and, as luck would have it, lay only a few feet below the surface. Most people believe that the Black Country owes its name to this coalfield. In addition to this coal, there were easily available deposits of ironstone, fireclay and limestone. This combination of minerals provided the natural wealth that a growing nation was able to exploit in order to take its turn in history's cycle as one of the dominant forces in the world.

The Black Country was and remained for the best part of two centuries the engine that has driven the way our world has chosen to occupy itself. It is safe to say that, without the discovery of easily available iron ore and coal in the Black Country, the Industrial Revolution would not have happened as it did. The fact that you and I expect to drive around in motor cars and get cross with the drivers of other motor cars who behave like complete pillocks; that we take for granted the aeroplanes we travel abroad on holiday in and get really brassed off when there is some unexplained delay in a flight we are waiting for; and that we assume that all things made from metal, like trains, ships, kettles, keys, kitchenware, and countersunk screws, just exist and will continue to exist shows how dependent we are on what happened in the forge we call the Black Country in the eighteenth and nineteenth centuries.

The people of the Black Country used to be known for being "strong in the arm but weak in the head" but now there's the University of Wolverhampton and it's the fifth biggest university in Britain. The Black Country became prosperous because it was the cauldron of manufacturing industry but now only a fifth of jobs are in manufacturing and twice as many people work in the service sector, doing things like answering the phone and delivering parcels. Two of the founder members of the Football League come from the Black Country but nowadays its sporting heroes are more likely to be found in kick-boxing, judo, javelin-throwing or netball while Wolverhampton Wanderers and West Bromwich Albion struggle out of the top ranks of football. Black Country people used to plan shopping expeditions to Birmingham, Cheltenham or London, but nowadays coachloads of people travel from Norwich, York, Gloucester, and even Birmingham itself to shop in Merry Hill, Dudley. The Black Country way of speaking used to be thought "common" but now there's Adrian Chiles, who anchors money programmes on television and radio with a distinctly Black Country accent, and Mark O'Shea, whose wildlife documentaries are not presented in the plummy tones of David Attenborough but in his own Wolverhampton voice.

Since the 1960s, roughly coinciding with the time when its industrial influence began to wane, there has been a significant growth in what I would call the Black Country "heritage industry". The Black Country Society was formed in 1966 with the aim of preserving and commemorating the life of this special part of England. Over the years it has been responsible for many events to celebrate the Black Country and produced a variety of interesting publications. Its quarterly magazine *'The Blackcountryman'* finds its way to the remotest parts of the world to which Black Country folk have emigrated. The Black Country Society's work eventually led to the creation in 1975 of the Black Country Museum in Dudley. The "heritage industry" was well and truly on its way!

I feel strangely ambivalent about all of this. On the one hand, I am quite keen to see my native territory promoted as more than the arsehole of England, as it has all too often been represented through its fictional characters. Remember Marlene - Beryl Reid's brilliantly-portrayed thick Midlander on radio? Or Benny - the equally thick bobble-hatted odd-job man in the Midlands' only ever soap opera, *Crossroads*? True, they were caricatures but where were the complementary positive characters? Can you imagine James Bond with a Black Country accent?

On the other hand, I am always slightly embarrassed at the romanticised and sanitised version of the Black Country that has begun to emerge, with its cast of quaint characters who were proud to work in this cradle of industry. I particularly dislike those books of grainy old photographs that seem to do a bomb in the shops. You know the sort of thing - men with baggy trousers and flat caps riding bicycles and women in long skirts with aprons over them walking down a tramlined street past handsome neo-Georgian buildings. I'm all for local pride but it has its dangers. The pretence behind these books of photographs is to portray a settled and happy time. It was nothing of the sort.

26

Still, we are all prone to want to believe in a past Golden Age.

Now, in my middle years, I have come to accept that the Black Country is the area which has infected and affected most of my life. It was time, therefore, that I came to some understanding of it before my left knee finally called it a day

TWO

THE BEST LAID PLANS

So, I decided to explore the Black Country but how was I to do it and how was I to report on my explorations?

I jettisoned a number of schemes, which included hitch-hiking around the area with a fridge (already done in Ireland), skateboarding along the area's pavements (too dangerous - and my daughters just laughed at the idea of someone my age on a skateboard), pedalling along the newly-laid cycleways around the areas' roads (tempting but I'm still not convinced that motorists actually understand all these cycle path markings), or simply catching buses from one town to the next and soaking up the atmosphere (too unreliable - you know what they say about buses!).

In the end, I decided that the most natural way to view the Black Country would be from the transportation routes that made it what it was - in other words its canals. And, since I'm still reasonably fit, despite this slightly wonky left kneecap which my doctor says won't need replacing for another twenty years, I thought I would walk along the canal towpaths. My plan was to complete a circular tour of the Black Country and to tell its story honestly.

This book then is an account of my journey on foot around the heart of the Black Country, following the towpaths of the canals which drove the area's development in the eighteenth and nineteenth centuries. It is my attempt to understand the land in which I made my first steps and which has made a significant contribution to who I am today.

I raided bookshops, libraries and the Internet to arm myself with an array of pamphlets, maps and web pages in order to plan my route. I quickly discovered that my plan was not as simple as I had at first thought. At the height of its activity, the Black Country canal system covered an amazing one hundred and sixty miles. In fact there were so many canals that the area was once described as "the Venice of England". Hard to believe, I know, but apparently it's true. Virtually all of these survived and were still in use throughout the nineteenth century and into the twentieth, despite the coming of the railways and the later arrival of the motor car. During the twentieth century, however, well over a third of the Black Country's canals have been lost - victims of infilling and overbuilding and sometimes of neglect.

And then came the "heritage industry"! Preservation groups have saved some canals and restored parts of others. To this very day they are planning to re-open stretches of canal that have been closed off for years. Dudley Council even has an official strategy for Dudley's canals, which puts great stress on the need to protect and preserve the canal network, its structures and its buildings as a valuable resource and a visible history of the community over the last three hundred years.

Enough of this nostalgia! One of the problems I have with the official version of the Black Country that is now so widely held is that it has put a romantic sheen over a past that was bloody, brutal and barbaric. The living and working conditions which people endured in the industrialised Black Country of the eighteenth and nineteenth centuries were generally appalling. Even now the mortality rate in Wednesbury is higher than in most other parts of England. The poor were exploited by the rich, of whom the richest were the Earls of Dudley whose family once lived in the area's outstanding historic landmark, Dudley Castle. It was successive Dudleys who ensured ownership of all the mineral rights in the Black Country by Enclosure Acts in the late eighteenth century. This made them extremely wealthy, which they remain to this day.

I want to give a picture of the Black Country as it is today, at the start of the twenty-first century. So, although I shall inevitably be drawing on the past to inform my narrative, I don't want to create the impression that the past is preferable to the present. Certainly it is another country but it is the country that lies underneath our present soil. It feeds that soil and it carries reminders. We can't do anything about that - we wouldn't be who we are today without it.

And that brings me back to my planned canal walk. From all the information I had gathered, I worked out a route which would take me around all of the major parts of the Black Country, give me time to visit sites I had a particular interest in and never have to retrace my steps. I would begin in Old Hill to the south and end in Stourbridge to the south west. Not quite a full circle but not far off. There were, however, two obstacles which I could see even then, some six months beforehand, that would cause me problems.

You see, the geography of the Black Country includes a ridge of high ground from Sedgley to Rowley Regis which the early canal-builders, or rather the manufacturers and mineral owners like the Earls of Dudley (yes, them again), had to find ways of traversing. So they built what was then an amazing construction - the two-mile Dudley Tunnel linking the canal systems of both sides of the town. Nearly sixty years later a second tunnel was built, over 3,000 yards long and known as the Netherton Tunnel, to relieve the congestion in the Dudley Tunnel.

Now you might think that these canal-builders had resolved my problem for me by building these two tunnels. After all, if you look at a map you can see how someone might do what I proposed, that is walk from Old Hill around the Black Country and finish in Stourbridge. But what you need to know, if you were for some reason daft enough to think of following in my footsteps, is that the Dudley Tunnel has no towpath, which makes walking it rather difficult! Actually I knew this already but had forgotten, because many years ago I went on a trip from our folk club in Sedgley which involved forty of us "legging" a narrow boat through the Dudley Tunnel. This was great fun but we then stupidly drank several pints of Banks's bitter before setting off on the return journey. You can imagine the difficulties of bladder control in the confined darkness underneath Dudley Castle! You don't need to know any more.

Nowadays the Dudley Tunnel is controlled by the Dudley Canal Trust and, when I rang them to enquire about getting on a "legging" boat for this part of my journey, I discovered that there were still trips for the length of the tunnel. Unfortunately, they went the wrong way.

Stymied!

While I was pondering on a solution to this problem, I thought I had better read about the second obstacle to my hoped-for smooth progress - the Netherton Tunnel. This sounded more like it, with a towpath on both sides and gas lighting along its length. Until I discovered that the gas lighting no longer worked. Daft of me to think it would really. After all, what's the point of lighting something that has no industrial use any longer? The guide books recommend that you take a torch but I decided I wanted more than a torch - I wanted a companion. Preferably someone who was big and strong, who would frighten off any marauding pirates or glue-sniffing youths met in the dark journey, and who was quiet and would be happy to let me think great thoughts without making me explain them all the time.

That was what I wanted.

What I got was John Gorman, former member of The Scaffold (remember *Lily the Pink*, and *Thank You Very Much for the Aintree Iron?*) and presenter on *Tiswas*. John at the time was Acting Unpaid Director of the Theatre-on-the-Steps in Bridgnorth, an old Shropshire market town some twelve miles from Wolverhampton where he and I had moved to live a few years previously. I've made it sound as though this was a joint choice. It wasn't. It was entirely coincidental. We had never met until I came to live in Bridgnorth and showed an interest in the Theatre-on-the-Steps. And this doesn't mean that I'm an actor; it means that I help behind the bar from time to time. Anyway, I was talking to John about my planned walk and about the suggestion made by my younger daughter who's done a course in marketing and therefore thinks she is an expert on these things. Her idea was that I might get some media interest in the walk if it was sponsored. And John came up with this brilliant idea of doing the walk in order to raise money for a feasibility study into Disabled Access to the Theatre-on-the-Steps.

Now John is no bigger or stronger than me, but he does have a very powerful voice. And I am actually quite solidly built, although I still feel myself to be the weedy teenager who avoided physical contests of strength like the plague. So I hoped that his voice and my bulk would be sufficient to get us an uninterrupted passage. By this stage I had found out that I could hire a boat for a private journey through the Dudley Tunnel and John hit on the second brilliant idea of selling tickets to some of the Bridgnorth luvvies for the trip.

And that's how, on 2nd April 2000 at exactly two o'clock in the afternoon, John and I came to be walking up to the entrance to the Dudley Tunnel.

THREE

THE VENICE OF ENGLAND

Before I get to the walk, however, I suppose I ought to start by getting some of this canal stuff out of the way first of all. Why were these waterways built at all?

It was money, of course, that drove their construction.

In the middle of the seventeenth century, there was this quirky bunch of entrepreneurs and inventors who had been attracted to the West Midlands area. At their heart was the Lunar Society, so called not because they were a bunch of weirdoes who went crazy at the full moon, but because its meetings were held at the full moon to make travel easier before the days of street lighting. They met to exchange information about experiments in the work-place, scientific discoveries and commercial opportunities. The Lunar Society's members included Matthew Boulton and James Watt, whose Soho Foundry was the world's first engineering works, Josiah Wedgwood, who founded the famous pottery works in Stoke, Erasmus Darwin, the grandfather of Charles Darwin and a noted evolutionist himself, Joseph Priestley, the noted chemist and theologist, and William Withering, who discovered the use of digitalis in the treatment of heart disease. Together they ensured the region's place at the forefront of the Industrial Revolution. In fact, the Black Country is the way it is today largely because of these "lunaticks"!

Now, the rapid growth of industrialisation depended on large quantities of coal being produced to fire the furnaces of this industry. Matthew Boulton, the leading "lunatick" and industrialist in the West Midlands area, heard from Wedgwood about the canal that James Brindley was hired to build in north Staffordshire to serve the pottery industry and he, with fellow-members of the Lunar Society, commissioned the same James Brindley to build a canal between Birmingham and the coal-fields of Wednesbury, right at the heart of the Staffordshire Thick Coal Seam. This first ten-mile stretch of what was to become the Birmingham Canal Navigations (or the BCN, as canal-anoraks call it) opened in 1769. Its opening more than halved the cost of coal in Birmingham and attracted new industries to its banks. By 1772 the BCN had been extended to beyond Wolverhampton, where it linked with the Staffordshire and Worcestershire Canal (the Staffs and Worcs in anorak-speak). Traffic grew and grew on the BCN, until in 1825 Thomas Telford chopped seven miles off Brindley's original meandering route by constructing huge cuttings, tunnellings and embankments thus reducing the number of rising and falling locks. The new BCN route was completed in 1838.

By the by, Thomas Telford had a busy life, eh? All those canals, bridges, and churches he built - I bet his back was sore afterwards. He even managed to finish the new BCN route three years after his death.

Meanwhile, Lord Dudley (yes, the same) was getting slightly miffed that he didn't have access to either the BCN, passing to the north-east of his castle, or to the Staffs and Worcs, passing to the south-west. The solution? Obvious really, if you're the exceedingly rich Lord Dudley. Build your own. And that's exactly what he did. Not personally, of course. You wouldn't catch the Dudleys getting their hands mucky but the engineer Thomas Dadford was employed to build the Stourbridge Canal, linking with the Staffs & Worcs at Stourton, and his dad, also called Thomas Dadford, was commissioned to build the Dudley Canal from Brierley Hill up to Dudley and, by what was a miracle for the time, under the town and castle via the Dudley Tunnel. The latter was completed in 1794 and was taken on to join up with the BCN at Tipton.

Its importance to Lord Dudley was that it connected with the underground tunnels to the limestone workings under the Wren's Nest and Dudley hills. And you know who owned all these workings, don't you!

Correct. Lord Dudley.

In 1798, a second Dudley Canal, quaintly christened Dudley No.2 to distinguish it from Dudley No.1, was opened from the south entrance to the Dudley Tunnel and linked up eventually with the Staffs & Worcs at Selly Oak, Birmingham. This cut was built purely to avoid the heavy tolls collected on the BCN. That's what privatisation does for you!

FOUR

BOSTIN' TALK

Up till now I have referred to these new waterways by the generally-used term canals. In the Black Country, they have never been known as canals; they are simply "cuts". And I do have to deal now with the matter of the way people speak in the Black Country, because if I don't you will get infuriated later on when you come across little bits of Black Country dialect as spoken by some native met on our journey.

It's really all the fault of that well-known dyke-digger Offa, King of the Mercians, and his cronies. For it was that Anglo-Saxon tribe, the Mercians, who settled this bit of central England between the fifth and seventh centuries and it is the remnants of the form of Old English spoken by these settlers that can still be heard in Black Country speech to this day. The sounds of this Old English survived the Danish and Norman invasions of England and many of these sounds transferred themselves into the written English of the fourteenth century, as we can see in the work of that period's pre-eminent poet, the writer who is usually thought of as the father of the English language – Geoffrey Chaucer.

This can be seen in the use of the prefix *a*-, as in *acoming* for *coming* or *afeard* for *afraid*, which Chaucer uses and which are still evident in Black Country speech. It is also seen in the suffix –en, as in *knowen* for *know* or *folken* for *folk*, used by Chaucer and still occasionally heard in the Black Country. These two usages are evident in a commonly used phrase in the Black Country *Am yow agooin?* for *Are you going*?

And that phrase brings in another strand of Black Country dialect, which is its unusual construction of the verb *to be* and the auxiliaries *have, do, can, shall, will* and *must*, especially when in their negative forms. Let's make a start with *to be*. The form *am* is used with all persons except he or she, so *you am*, *we am* and *they am* are normal usages. In fact, just to prove this, the giant toy store TOYS 'R' US, which opened in Oldbury some years ago, is known locally as TOYS AM WE. So one linguistic joke is piled on to another.

Similar constructions are found in other dialects which, like Black Country, are remnants of older speech patterns in Anglo-Saxon settlers. What is highly unusual, however, and not found in any other dialect is the disappearance of the negative form *not*. So in the Black Country *I ay* or, confusingly, *I bay* means *I am not*; *I day* means *I did not*; *I cor* means *I cannot*; *I shor* means *I shall not*; *I wor* means *I was not*; *I doh* means *I do not*; and *I woh* means *I will not*.

Now, if you've got hold of the stuff about negatives, you're well on your way to understanding Black Country speech, but there's still the problem of sounds or accent. I've already used the spelling *yow* for *you* – a spelling that Chaucer used to represent the pronunciation of the word in his day. *Yow* has its origins in the Anglo-Saxon *eow*, just as *yower* for *your* comes from Anglo-Saxon *eower*. There are lots of other examples where the vowel sounds of the Black Country are at variance with those spoken by those would-be preservers of posh speaking, the Queen's English Society. Frequently, the short *a* sound becomes a short *o*, as in *'ommer* for *hammer* (there are no aspirates in the Black Country) or *loff* for *laugh*. An extension of this is when a similar vowel sound becomes a short *o*, seen when *horse* becomes *'oss*. At other times the *o* sound becomes *a*, as in *shap* for *shop* or *drap* for *drop*. Sometimes the more clipped vowels of contemporary English are stretched, as in *maerk* for *make* or *waerk* for *work* (compare this with Anglo-Saxon *weorc* and Chaucer's *werke*).

There are also lots of Anglo-Saxon words which have hung around

37

for centuries, used with equal fluency by the original settlers and by Chaucer and by modern-day Black Country speakers. These include *ax* (Anglo-Saxon *axian*, Chaucer *axe*) for *ask*, *lairn* (Anglo-Saxon *laeran*, Chaucer *lerne*) for *learn*, *wusser* (Anglo-Saxon *wyrsa*, Chaucer *wurs*) for *worse*, *betterer* (Anglo-Saxon *betera*, Chaucer *bettre*) for *better*, and many others. A key Black Country word, *bostin*, which tends to be used indiscriminately in praise of anything that someone really likes, comes from the Anglo-Saxon *bogan* and then the Chaucerian *bosten* meaning *to boast about*. Another common Black Country expression, *blart*, meaning *to cry like a baby*, shows how vowel sounds have shifted around over centuries. Its Anglo-Saxon equivalent is *blaeren* but in Chaucer's time it was written as *blaren* or *bleren* or *bloren*.

So, let's try a little bit of Black Country dialogue to see if you've got hold of all this.

'Am yow agooin to wairk tomorrer?'

'I ay. I'm agooin shappin. They've got some bostin 'ommers up Brummagem. D'yow fancy comin?'

'I cor.'

'Goo on. It'll be a loff.'

'Doh be saft. Yow woh get paid.'

' I doh care. I need a new 'ommer.'

Thus did Black Country folk discuss the minutiae of their lives over the garden fence, while the furnaces glowed in the sky behind them, belching out black smoke into the atmosphere, and the navvies dug the cuts in the valley below them. And thus they still speak.

Black Country speech is most commonly found in the stories of two apocryphal local characters known as Aynuk and Ayli, who stem

from that nineteenth century tradition of naming child
characters, in this case Enoch and Eli. Aynuk and Ayl[i]
in the Black Country. The two are characters of some[v]
to whom events happen which they are a bit slow to
an example:

Aynuk was walking along the cut one day when he heard a cry for
help coming from the water. Aynuk looked around and spotted a bloke
drowning. Instead of helping him out, Aynuk ran along the cut bank,
up a road and through a factory gate. He rushed up to the foreman
and said:
'I've just sid Jack Edwards drowning in the cut. Can I 'ave 'is job?'
'Sorry, Aynuk,' says the foreman, 'I've just gid it the bloke what
pushed 'im in.'

And here's another:

Aynuk and Ayli were strolling along the cut and they had a bit of an
argument and eventually started shouting at each other.
'If yow doh shurrup,' says Aynuk. 'I'll chuck yow across the cut.'
'I bet yow a quid yow cor do it,' says Ayli.
Next minute Aynuk picks Ayli up, twirls him round his head several
times, then lets him go. Ayli falls into the middle of the cut.
'See,' says Ayli. 'I told yow yow couldn't do it. Yow owe me a quid.'
'I doh,' says Aynuk. 'I day say I could do it fust time.'

Black Country folk tell these stories with relish and with a sense
of self-mockery. They know that the world at large tends to look down
on them and the way they speak but they are not stupid. They know that

be quite useful at times to play up to this stereotype because, en they show unexpected perceptiveness, they are able to surprise those who hold this narrow view of them.

I think Black Country speech is wonderful. It has rhythm, it has character, it has great strength. It is one of those things that make the Black Country unique and I wish my schooling had not deprived me of it. It has greater validity in my opinion than the standard English that arose from our Norman conquerors from across "the wairter". This is widely known in the Black Country and it is why more recent incomers from Bangladesh or Bosnia, from the Caribbean or the Caucasus, from Pakistan or Poland, from India or from Ireland, insist that their children speak with the voice of Aynuk and Ayli, even when those children hear nothing in their homes but the language their parents bring with them.

I have sketched the dialect of the Black Country briefly and as if it were a common form throughout the region. It is not. There are variations between towns and between different parts of the Black Country. An expert (of which there are plenty in the Black Country) can tell the difference between a Wednesbury voice and a Netherton one, or a Bilston voice and a West Bromwich one. But I am running ahead of myself because I have not introduced you to any of these places yet. So I hope that this brief description of our language has tickled your fancy even more and that you are dying to join us on our trip.

I'll just leave you with one more Aynuk and Ayli story and then, I promise, no more.

Aynuk on return from his first visit to the seaside, tells Ayli that he had 'sid an iron boat sairlin' on the say'.
'Doh be saft, Aynuk,' said Ayli. 'It 'ud sink.'
'I tell yow it day sink,' insisted Aynuk.

So, when he gets home, in order to prove whether Aynuk was right or wrong, Ayli throws the iron bedstead into the cut. And, of course, it sinks.

Next day, Ayli sees Aynuk and says to him:

'I thort yow told me that an iron boat day sink. Well, I've chucked th' ode bedstead in the cut and it went strairt to the bottom.'

'Goo on, yow fewel,' says Aynuk. 'Doh yow know yow gorrave salt wairter?'

Which brings me back to Sunday April 2nd and the distinctly unsalty water of the Dudley No.1 Canal as it enters the two-mile Dudley Tunnel.

FIVE

THE GENTLE FOLK OF STOURBRIDGE

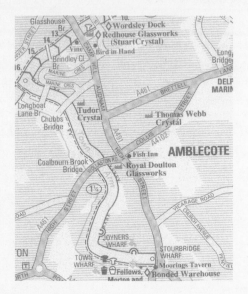

Actually, we didn't start at the "legging" tunnel. We started in Stourbridge, at the end of the Stourbridge arm of the Stourbridge Canal by a building that is known as The Bonded Warehouse. This was built in the heyday of the canals and its bottom floor used to be open to the canal so that boats could unload and trade there. Imagine a submarine, captained by James Bond, surfacing in Goldfinger's headquarters - maybe that's where the term Bonded came from!

You see, once I had decided to involve John and to try to raise money for disabled access to our little theatre in Bridgnorth, the nature of the expedition began to shift perceptibly. We were now looking to draw as much media attention as we could get to what we were doing.

What could be better, we reasoned as we spent the winter months planning, rather like Scott must have spent time musing in advance of his Antarctic Expedition, than to set off at a time when we were most likely to attract attention? And what better, we furthermore reasoned, than having a gang of luvvies and luvvie-associates, especially some that were disabled, to help us "leg" through the Dudley Tunnel?

Anyway, the impact of all these months of careful preparation was that the walk started in Stourbridge, not in Old Hill as I had originally planned, and the route was exactly reversed from the one I had so carefully prepared first of all. No matter, we could still cover the heart of the Black Country and I could see all I wanted to see.

And then we chose a Sunday afternoon which turned out to be Mother's Day, when large numbers of possible fellow-leggers were tied to their families. It also turned out to be the day when England were to meet Scotland at the conclusion of the Six Nations Rugby Championshiops, and F.A. Cup semi-final day when Aston Villa were to play Bolton Wanderers. That just about accounted for anyone from the local media who we might have enticed to come and see us off.

Clever, eh?

So, Stourbridge it was where we started.

Stourbridge folk don't really like to think of themselves as coming from the Black Country. They really hated it when they were placed in Dudley under local government reorganisation in 1974 and there's a group of them still arguing for independence. You see Stourbridge used to be in Worcestershire and many of its residents would prefer to see themselves as country gentlefolk. There are more Stourbridge residents in social classes A/B/C1 than probably anywhere else in the Black Country. And that's not counting those who escaped to Hagley, just outside Stourbridge, which just *loves* being still part of Worcestershire,

43

where proper gentlefolk dwell. You know Stourbridge is a bit posh because it's the only place in the Black Country that's got a Waitrose supermarket. Rumour has it that, to this day, there are people digging a tunnel under the Clent Hills to enable more Stourbridge folk to escape to Worcestershire without being noticed (and to sneak back into Waitrose for their weekly shopping!).

The Bonded Warehouse at the end of the cut stands just beyond the Stourbridge ring road which is a race-track for soft-top Saabs and tinted-glass Beamers, driven by forty-five-year-old boy racers in baseball caps and designer stubble. This encircles Stourbridge town centre and is the reason why the latter is known colloquially as "The Bubble". Within "The Bubble" is quite an attractive old town, including the Talbot Hotel, which used to be the residence of the Foley family who were one of the most powerful local ironmasters in the seventeenth and eighteenth centuries. The dynasty was begun by one Richard Foley, known as Fiddler Foley because he is reputed to have travelled to Sweden pretending to be an idiot and playing the fiddle. There he made friends with Swedish ironworkers and thus discovered how a slitting mill worked. On his return to Stourbridge, he set up his own slitting mill, which was an important step in the development of one of the ancient Black Country trades of nailmaking.

"The Bubble" also houses King Edward VI Sixth Form College, among whose former scholars are Dr. Samuel Johnson of dictionary fame and Robert Plant of Led Zeppelin fame.

Now Dr. Johnson is dead, of course, and his dictionary didn't promise much by way of companionship so we tried to get Robert Plant to come with us on this first part of our walk. Unfortunately, he was busy elsewhere on the day in question so I myself had to point out to John the Stourbridge Ironworks that we passed on the first bend of the towpath. This is where the world's first ever steam engine, *The Stourbridge Lion*, was built for use in Pennsylvania hauling coal from the mines. *The Lion* was only used in an 1829 trial in America and never commercially. Mind you, its remains have been preserved in the Smithsonian Museum in Washington, so Americans must think it important, although local folk are bemused by this fact. Another locomotive, *The Agenoria*, also made in this factory, ferried coal on the Kingswinford line from the same time for thirty years. It is now housed in the National Railway Museum in York.

'Is that why Planty played in a heavy metal band?' John wanted to know.

I chose not to answer him. This is what comes of going on an expedition with a man who made a career as a comedian!

The first stages of our journey took place in drizzly conditions and we needed our waterproof jackets on. We passed the occasional fisherman, tented underneath a huge green umbrella and surrounded by that special fisherman's paraphernalia of four types of maggot, six types of rod and twenty-three types of hook.

'Have you noticed with fishermen that they all wear that same expression?' John said.

This was clearly a topic he had strong views on for some reason.

'It's as if they had had a really bad experience over the breakfast table. Or they're badly constipated.'

I was anxious that one of the fishermen we were passing would turn round and wallop him. And me. So I answered non-committally.

'It certainly doesn't look to be much fun what they're doing.'

Minutes later we were passed, in the opposite direction, by a couple of pitter-pattering joggers, out for their Sunday morning constitutionals, and a group of mountain bikers of indeterminate age swaddled in skintight lycra and hiding behind wrap-around yellow dayglo glasses. Proper mountain bikers ride up mountains, of course, but there aren't any mountains in Stourbridge so this bunch were just having a nice n' easy spin along the towpath. I suspect that the spatterings of mud that flecked their faces and the backs of their legs had come from spray-on cans (only available in Waitrose, of course).

Where the Stourbridge Arm meets the main Stourbridge Canal we came upon our first, and, as it turned out, our only, narrowboat of the day. The couple uncertainly manoeuvring it through the lock had just bought the boat and were taking it back home to somewhere south of Watford. It looked a bit of a dodgy venture, when it was us they were asking about how to open the lock gates. We knew even less about the operation than they did. But *we* had an excuse. *We* were walking the cuts. *They* were supposed to be boating on them!

The lock they were struggling with was the first (or last if you're travelling the other way) of the Stourbridge Sixteen, as canal-anoraks refer to them. These are a set of rising locks that begin taking the cut from the low levels of the Staffordshire plain up towards Dudley town. Two locks further on brought us to the Glasshouse Bridge underneath the old turnpike road, where we passed right next to the imposing, hundred-foot high Redhouse Glass Cone of Stuart Crystal.

SIX

THE CRYSTAL MAZE

Stourbridge is known worldwide for its glass industry, which was begun in the early seventeenth century by Huguenot glassmakers who had come to England from their native Lorraine in France to escape religious persecution. In the guidebooks, which were probably written by someone from Stourbridge, they are usually described as "gentlemen glassmakers". In fact, although they were certainly descended from the minor French aristocracy, they had been moving around England for over a hundred years - the New Age travellers of their time - shifting on when the charcoal fires they needed for their glass-making could no longer be fuelled from the surrounding woodlands.

After trying a number of other sites in England, these medieval hippies were attracted to the Stourbridge area by the plentiful and easily available coal and fireclay for their furnaces. And there they settled. They built the first glasshouse in Stourbridge in 1618 but they would not have survived had it not been for the timely invention of lead glass sixty years later. This led to the huge growth of the Stourbridge glass industry in the eighteenth and nineteenth century and for the crystal glassware which is still an important industry of the area. At one time the area around Stourbridge looked like the moon's surface, dotted with glasshouse cones, but today the industry is represented chiefly by Webb Corbett, Royal Doulton and Stuart Crystal, whose cone is one of four remaining in the country.

Lots of people have got some of this lead crystal staring down at them from a shelf or carefully locked away in a cupboard and kept for best. Which probably means that they only use it at Christmas, if at all.

That's certainly the case in the Black Country, because Stourbridge lead crystal is a favourite gift for weddings, christenings, anniversaries, retirements and so forth. The irony is that most of it is bought as seconds, because it's so much cheaper and you can't really see the faults, and then it's treated reverentially as if it was the family silver!

Dudley Council, busy developing Dudley as a tourist attraction, recognises the importance of the crystal glass industry and there is a well signposted Glass Tour that takes motorists around major sites. One of these is the Broadfield House Glass Museum in Kingswinford, which houses an interesting collection of glass from the eighteenth century to the present-day. It is situated no more than a mile from the canalside by the Glasshouse Bridge, so we dutifully trekked there only to find it is only open in the afternoons. We pressed our noses to the window and could see lots of glass and some of it looked very attractive. Maybe if you're a glass-anorak it all makes sense, but I couldn't quite see what it was all about. It wasn't my cup of tea. Or should I say glass of wine?

But Kingswinford leads me nicely into the Black Country's role in the Gunpowder Plot.

The Gunpowder Plot, as not many people in the United Kingdom know, was a scheme by Catholics to get rid of Parliament and to rescind the Protestantism that had been established by Henry VIII. Its leader, of course, was Guy Fawkes and he attempted to blow up the Houses of Parliament on November 5th, 1605, which is why we have the annual Bonfire Night celebrations on that date. Personally I've never been very sure what it is we are celebrating - is it the fact that Guy Fawkes failed in his mission, so preserving a Protestant state? Or is it that we wish he had succeeded and that we might thus have been rid of parliament and all its works?

Anyway, the reason for bringing all this in is that some of the

Catholic conspirators were actually from the Black Country. Well, they weren't *exactly* from the Black Country, but they certainly spent time there when they were in flight after poor old Guy Fawkes failed in his plan. The main man was Robert Catesby who, with some of his co-conspirators, hid out at the home of his pal Stephen Lyttleton at Holbeache House, near Himley. This is just down the road from Broadfield House Glass Museum and so provides a pretty feeble excuse for me to bring this matter into my narrative. Sadly, Catesby and some of his pals were found and killed at Holbeache House but Lyttleton and Robert Winter escaped and skulked around Rowley Regis and Hagley for a while till they too were arrested and subsequently hung, drawn and quartered for treason in London.

So there we are! That was probably the closest that the Black Country came to changing national history until the beginnings of the Industrial Revolution.

Anyway, we missed the Glass Museum but we did climb up from the cut to have a look inside the Redhouse Cone, which claims to be "the only preserved 200 year old glassmaking cone in the United Kingdom". The Cone is no longer used for glassmaking but has been turned into a sort of working museum where the traditional skills of glassmakers ("passed down from generation to generation") are demonstrated and where the old pot furnace and other tools of the trade are on display.

This was the scene of our second setback in as many hours. It didn't bode well.

At first, when we reached the roadside and saw the sign advertising "Sunday opening at 10.00 a.m.", we thought we were just a few minutes early. Even when we saw that the Cone itself was wreathed in scaffolding, we didn't give it more than a moment's thought. But, when we tried to push open the gates, we received a frosty admonition from a woman in uniform who informed us that we couldn't come in because the Redhouse Cone was closed.

'What time will it open?' I queried innocently.

'In twelve months,' she snapped.

There's no answer to that! My great scheme to show John the marvels of the Black Country was already on shaky ground. All that meticulous planning, all that reading, all those months of plotting our route and the sites we were to visit. And the first two we came to weren't open! My itinerary for the day was already blown off course. I had allowed an hour or more for us to tour the Redhouse Cone and now what were we to do?

There was nothing for it but to continue on our journey.

SEVEN

"GOO TO BRIERLEY HILL"

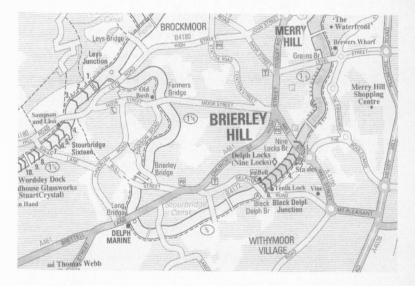

Back on the towpath we climbed steadily up towards Brierley Hill, passing the last twelve locks of the Stourbridge Sixteen. There is a wealth of helpful information at various points on this stretch of the cut, provided by maps and interpretation notices, telling us about the glass industry and other noteworthy features of the canal. This part of our walk, less than a mile in total, is one of the most attractive stretches, despite the fact that it goes through areas where there is evidence of heavy industrial activity. Several now-unused basins and weirs bear testimony to their past use but have now been colonised by a variety of vegetation and wildlife, including a chirpy family of ducks who swam merrily alongside us as we walked.

We kept to the Stourbridge Canal at the Leys Junction and headed in a loop around Brierley Hill. In this section the water was full of beer-cans, plastic bottles, dead bikes and other junk where the long gardens of old council houses reach down to the waterside on the opposite side to the towpath. Sadly, most of these garden-ends are neglected, although occasionally there is evidence that some householder has realised the potential of the canalside and planted attractive bushes or flowers. Every garden-end, however, has its own ancient plastic chair facing the cut, in which once upon a time someone has sat and contemplated the mysteries of the universe. Or had a fag.

We were now well ahead of schedule so, when we reached Black Delph Bridge, we decided to go for a cup of coffee in one of the local pubs. The one we chose is called The Tenth Lock, for reasons that will shortly become apparent. Of course, it was Sunday, wasn't it? And it too was closed, so we had to press on without our coffee.

The final rise up to Brierley Hill was past the spectacular Delph Locks, which take the cut from Black Delph where the Stourbridge Canal and the Dudley No.1 Canal meet. These are known as the Nine Locks, though there are actually, and typically for the Black Country, only eight of them after rebuilding work in the middle of the nineteenth century (hence The Tenth Lock we failed to get into). They are very close together and the view back down them from the top is magnificent, stretching out towards the Shropshire and Welsh borderland. In the nineteenth century and for the early part of the twentieth such views would have been virtually impossible to catch through the fug of industrial smoke and the soot from collieries. But it is not impossible to imagine the bargemen looking back in wonder at this magnificent piece of engineering.

But we were cold by now and so we followed the towpath signs to Merry Hill and came up at the Copthorne Hotel, where we decided to take coffee. Breakfast was being cleared away as we sat down so we had a short wait in the bar area while fresh coffee was brewed. The décor in the bar of this plush modern hotel is really quite bizarre. The ceiling is decorated in a classical art fashion with huge figures of men and women in flowing robes and cherubs clutching pots, while hanging over the dining tables are replicas of hot-air balloons and World War 1 aeroplanes. At the far end, the walls are decorated with Victorian-style gilt-edged pictures of pastoral scenes, while plaster models of black jazz musicians, chefs and, for some inexplicable reason, policemen stand on every available raised surface. And then, there was a TV screen above the bar showing a silent Sky News, while Carpenters' muzak lulled us as we sat drying off.

'Someone got paid for designing all this,' said John, who thinks himself a bit of an expert on all things arty.

'Not very much by the look of things,' I rejoined wittily.

He gave me one of those old-fashioned looks which was designed to remind me that he was the funny one here. I grinned weakly back.

Still, the coffee was nice.

It was now midday, so we retraced our steps a short distance, climbing up to the road from the towpath at Nine Locks Bridge, in order to get to our lunchtime stopping point at one of the Black Country's best-known pubs - The Bull and Bladder.

Now, to strangers, this causes some confusion because the name displayed on the outside of the building, underneath the painted "Blessing of Your Heart: You Brew Good Beer", a quotation from Shakespeare's *Two Gentlemen of Verona*, is The Vine. But everyone locally knows it as The Bull and Bladder and, like so many things in the Black Country, there are two explanations for this soubriquet.

The official one is that the place was originally a butcher's shop kept by two eccentric brothers, Joseph and James Atwood, who occasionally served home-brewed beer. After their death the shop was sold in 1905 to Daniel and Caleb Batham, who were members of a local brewing family. Extensive reconstruction was required due to mining subsidence but the building that stands now has stood pretty much as it was for nearly a hundred years. And, although it has been a pub all that time, it has allegedly retained the name of The Bull and Bladder from its time as a butcher's shop.

A more direct explanation is that the "bull" is what comes out of people's mouths after drinking Batham's beer and the "bladder" is what processes that beer on its way to the urinals.

The Vine, with its fond nickname, is now the cornerstone of the Batham's operation with its nine Black Country pubs which are known as The Batham's Nine. There is a totally illegal and totally unadvertised tour of all these pubs. It's done by bicycle and you only get to go on it by invitation. It requires you to drink a pint of Batham's beer in every one of the nine pubs, cycling between each of them before returning to the Bull and Bladder. Grown men have been known to accomplish this feat on their sons' Chopper bikes, believe it or not, while other grown men have been known to find their legs turning to jelly as they try to cycle between the seventh and eighth pub. The famous Delph Brewery, situated in the adjoining building, continues to produce Delph dark mild ale and the exquisite Batham's bitter which in 1991 was voted winner of the best bitter category at the Great British Beer Festival organised by the Campaign for Real Ale.

The original plan had been to have something to eat in the Bull and Bladder because it has a reputation for doing the best-value sandwiches in the Midlands, if not the world. Thick bread, filled with whatever meat and salad you fancy, for a quid. I've been before and they are exquisite. What I hadn't realised, of course, was that this service is only available during the week and not on Sundays. The room I took John into where they normally make the sandwiches was empty, except for its noticeboards proclaiming it to be the meeting place of the local branch of the Royal Order of the Antediluvian Buffaloes – a kind of working men's masonic brotherhood. So, we had to be content with a tasty pint of Batham's bitter, the finest beer in the universe, and a seat among the other Sunday lunchtime regulars in the bar, moaning about all the things they normally moan about on Sundays and probably on every other day of the week.

Then, refreshed and relaxed but in need of food, we rejoined the towpath where we had left it and very soon we were looking down at that Mecca of Retail Therapy - Merry Hill.

EIGHT

MERRY HELL

Now, read any book about the West Midlands cuts or about the Black Country and you'll generally find a big gap just about here. You see, Merry Hill, or Merry Hell as the locals call it, is everything that heritage-anoraks hate. It's bold, it's brash, it's modern; its denizens don't wear cloth caps and neckerchiefs, they don't drink tea out of quaint multi-coloured jugs, and they don't give a monkey's about the past. It was built on the site of a former and much-lamented steelworks, where generations of (mostly) men had done proper Black Country work in metal-bashing. It's also a monument to the thrusting, in-your-face, no-such-thing-as-society, late flowering of capitalism in the nineteen-eighties under that bossyboots Maggie Thatcher.

The trouble is that this snobbery about Merry Hill doesn't quite stack up. First of all, the Round Oak steelworks which had previously been on the site were closed in 1982 but they had been losing jobs for several years prior to that time as demand for British steel declined in the face of cheaper production elsewhere in the world. The site lay empty for almost two years as Dudley Council tried unsuccessfully to find a buyer for it. Eventually, two local property developers, the twins Don and Roy Richardson, themselves born and brought up in Brierley Hill, were invited to submit their ideas on regenerating the area.

The redevelopment of the hundred and twenty-five acres, which began in late 1984 and took several years to complete, transformed the original site. Thousands of tonnes of earth were bulldozed and the foundations of the original steelworks were crushed and used for road and parking construction. Merry Hell now has over two hundred and twenty stores, which include Debenhams, Marks and Spencer, Sainsbury's, Asda, C & A, Boots and Argos, twenty-eight catering outlets with a total of over two thousand seats, and it attracts over twenty million visitors per year, an average of 385,000 per week. Over half of these consumers come from outside the Black Country.

Here is some more really useful information from the Merry Hell web-site:

- Merry Hell's busiest month is December. Its busiest day is the first day of sales after Christmas.

- Visitors spend more than two hours per visit.

- Merry Hell employs in excess of 4000 staff.

- Merry Hell has 7,000 car parking spaces on site.

- Between the hours of 11 a.m. and 2 p.m. Merry Hell has ninety-eight buses per hour driving through its bus station.

Fascinating stuff, eh? This is what they put on the Internet to entice shoppers. Are we enticed?

To many people (including my elder daughter) Merry Hell is Paradise, El Dorado, sheer bliss, Utopia, very heaven, kingdom come, the Elysian Fields, and that's exhausted my computer's thesaurus.

I was all for popping into Merry Hell and, although John was a quaint old heritage-anorak on this issue, I persuaded him that we could buy a sandwich there. I also promised to show him the other delights of the centre.

'John, you just have to see the traditional Merry Hell costume,' I tried. 'It's fabulous.'

'What's that then?' he asked. I thought I had him interested.

'There's two sorts of people who frequent Merry Hell,' I began. 'The young and the old. And, among the young there's two types of acceptable kit, one for the women and one for the blokes. Mind you, when I say young, you have to take that term loosely. It means those that think they're young. At least among the women.'

'Go on,' he said, though I could see I wasn't impressing him too much.

'Well, the Full Monty for women is the bottle-blonde hair with the dark roots just showing and the sunglasses woven in, the tight-fitting skirt and top in whatever the latest fashionable colour is, the high-heeled white-leather shoes, the crimson-lipped mouth and the long, flickering eyelashes. And all this has to be paraded in style through the shopping malls. So there's a practised bum wiggle, a quickstep scissoring as they walk, a constant clocking of passing males to check whether the eyes have swivelled, and a regular checking of the make-up in shop windows.'

'Know what you mean,' John said. 'We call them slappers in Liverpool.'

'Then there's the young blokes,' I continued unabashed. 'And they usually are young. Their chosen attire is the puffa jacket, whatever the weather, worn over shiny Adidas track-suit bottoms and a lumberjack shirt flapping over the trousers. They have Oasis-type basin-haircuts, greased down, or shaven heads, and they glower a lot to look hard. And there's something else you have to have if you're a real Merry Heller.'

'What's that?'

'A mobe, of course,' I explained. 'You can't be seen dead in Merry Hell if you're under thirty without a mobile phone clamped to your ear as you go round. I'm convinced that most of them are just talking to their mates at the other end of the Mall.'

'Some of them are just talking to themselves,' John said. 'Those who can't afford the rental. Haven't you got a mobile phone?'

At this point I have to explain something.

Three years ago, because I was working in what is laughingly known as a "mobile situation", in other words I was having to drive around England a lot as part of my work and never knew when - or if - I would get home and therefore felt responsible to those who cared about me, I bought a mobile phone. Yes, I know, I'd sat irritated on trains listening to Mobies in their loud voices telling someone at the office that they were on the train; I'd seen young people wandering around towns that I knew well, like Wolverhampton and Dudley, with mobes stuck to their ears as if they were receiving instructions on how to walk; I'd pontificated in the pub like every other middle-aged bore about how I wasn't surprised that Mobies were getting deadly rays from their mobes which would sooner or later turn them into gibbering idiots like extraterrestials in *Dr.Who* or *Star Trek*.

Yes, I'd done all that. But still I bought myself a mobe.

And, though it pains me to say it, it was in fact extremely useful. I sussed it all out first, of course. Bought *Which* magazine to find the best value for money. Borrowed a mate of mine's to see if I could work the damn thing. Took copies of all the advertising gubbins home to peruse, in the daft belief that I would understand any of the technical bumf. I mean, does anybody, even a proper Mobie, understand all that stuff? D'you know what pulse dialling is? I thought it was something to do with using the inside of your wrist. And telephony? Come on! The manuals they give you once you do decide to part with your hard-earned are the give-away. They're all written in several languages and you know, you just know, that the one they were written in first wasn't English. In fact, given the shape of the world's economy at present, they were probably written in Korean or maybe even Gaelic. And what you get is some Korean's or Gael's attempt at a translation.

Anyway, despite all of this, I eventually convinced myself that I needed a mobe and so I bought one. From British Telecom, of course. Well, they used to be a public corporation so I reasoned that you could probably trust them more.

Daft, eh?

But the reason I'm mentioning all of this is because twelve months ago I decided that I didn't need the mobe any longer. You don't need to know the whys and wherefores, but I didn't. So I found a phone number on one of my bills and rang to cancel. Well, that was a right game, I can tell you. I couldn't cancel there and then because I had to give a month's notice or something like that. Fair enough, I thought. I'd expected some snag. You get inured to this sort of thing in the modern thrusting United Kingdom plc. So I bit my tongue as I listened to the steps I would have to take to get rid of my mobe and how and when I would have to settle my final bill.

And then Liam or whatever his name was, who was explaining all this to me, suddenly asked:

'What is the reason why you are giving up your mobile phone?'

Cheeky prat! I thought to myself, then decided to voice this *bon mot*.

'Don't be such a cheeky prat!' I said victoriously, feeling proud of myself for taking on these voices of darkness.

But he carried on relentlessly.

'Is it because you are switching to another provider?' he asked.

'No.'

'Is it because you are dissatisfied with British Telecom's service?'

'No.'

'Is there some other reason?'

'Yes.'

'Would you be prepared to divulge to British Telecom what your reason is.'

'No.'

And there was an embarrassed pause. No doubt Liam was thinking of going to ask his manager for further guidance but I decided I would save him the trouble.

'I don't want to deal with prats like you any longer,' I said. ' Why don't you get yourself a proper job? Instead of sitting there answering telephones all day long. When I was your age....'

Liam, or whoever, had the foresight to put the phone down at that point.

The other regular clientele at Merry Hell is the old folk, the pensioners, the senior citizens, the past-sixty and past-caring. Remember how public libraries used to have reading rooms stuffed with old men pretending to read *The Financial Times* or *The Daily Torygraph*, when all they were doing was keeping out of the cold? Well, Merry Hell and shopping malls like it have replaced libraries for this purpose. They are under cover, spacious and heated. There are plenty of shop windows to look at and plenty of wooden benches to sit on and watch the bottle-blondes and the basin-cuts hurrying by, holding their interminable conversations with their mobes. You don't have to pretend to be reading anything.

And, even better, you can get the pensioners' special breakfast from the Asda caff, which is served Monday to Friday from 9.00 a.m. onwards, so the only people you have to fight for a place in the queue are old farts like yourself. Then you can take your tasty selection of five items for £1.59 from bacon, sausage, fried egg, beans, tomatoes, fried bread, scrambled egg, hash browns, and sit down at one of those lovely formica-topped tables. There, being sure to keep your overcoat, hat and scarf firmly on, you can tuck in whilst simultaneously moaning about anything that takes your fancy - the government, the price of a glass of Guinness or of bri-nylon underpants, the sheer daftness of mobile phones, how nothing tastes as good as it used to, Camilla and Charles, or the buses.

Wonderful, isn't it?

Who could have imagined that life would ever be like this? Free light and heat all day AND a proper English breakfast for £1.59.

We didn't go to the Asda caff. We bought a sandwich and sat on a bench overlooking some escalators and sat there munching. A woman sitting next to us said she'd heard there was a lot of walking to do in Merry Hell but she hadn't realised you had to wear hiking boots! No one else noticed us. The crowds milled around us, behind us, and up and down the escalators, intent on their retail therapy. So we finished our sandwiches, took off all our clothes, and walked stark naked through the malls until we reached the exit to the road back up to the canalside.

Actually, that last bit isn't true. But it might just as well have been. There we were, dressed in waterproof cagoules and hiking boots, with rucksacks on our backs and maps in hands, and no one paid the slightest attention to us. You'd think that they were used to seeing polar explorers.

The last part of the Merry Hell complex we passed through on the cut side was the section which attracts office workers at lunchtimes and the young trendsetters of Dudley in the evenings. A series of eating places has been created which face out to the expensively-refurbished cut basin. Here you can choose from Greek, Chinese, Indian, American or English restaurants and café-bars, mostly staffed by young people chosen for their outgoing and chirpy approach to life. That sort of service is a real and refreshing change from the glowering resentful service you used to get in English eating places. The food isn't always as bright and chirpy, alas.

Some of that day's lunching office workers were no doubt on a break from the call centre for Egg, the Prudential Assurance Company's new telephone banking centre. Now, I have developed a thing about call centres and about the way that their staff have been trained to deal with you. Have you ever thought about the instruction sheet that their staff's telephone voices read from:

'Hello, you're through to Egg. My name is Tracy. How can I help you?'

'I've got something I want to put into your Egg.'

'Thank you, sir. Would that be a short-term, medium-term or long-term insertion, sir?'

'Depends how many pints of Batham's I've had first, doesn't it?'

'Thank you, sir. Bear with me and I'll just ask my manager.'

Then comes the cheerful music. If you're lucky, it's something you might vaguely feel able to hum along to. An instrumental version of a Beatles melody, for instance, played by someone who has clearly had some kind of training in the use of the Moog synthesiser. But more than likely, you'll be unlucky and have some God-awful rendition of Carpenters' muzak, played by some demented twelve-year-old on an electronic keyboard given as a present last Christmas.

They always say "Bear with me" before they cut you off. When we were moving into our new house some two years ago and having to negotiate telephone numbers, electricity and gas connections, the final minutiae of a mortgage agreement, the exact times when removal persons would arrive, the great handing over of the keys ceremony with the solicitor and so on, my wife and I counted that we were asked to "Bear with me" three thousand, two hundred and six times exactly. Honest.

Why do they do this, these telephone girls (for they are always girls)? I have an image in my head of this army of bottle-blonde twenty-year-olds who are trained by some middle-aged matron on a parade ground somewhere just south of Lincoln to say "Bear with me" in that ingratiating, irritating tone, so that they can then put the phone down, reach for a packet of Silk Cut and turn to their neighbouring bottle-blonde to say, through a cloud of exhaled smoke:

'Got another of them clever prats on, Jude,'

'Oh, yeah,' will come the reply.

'You had one today?'

'Yeah. I had two this morning. Bleeding perves! Makes you wanna puke. You coming out tonight?'

'Where?'

'Going to the Black Country Museum. They've got a bit of a do on. Rug-podging. Fancy it?'

'Nah! Got to do me hair.'

Then they each pick up the phone and say, simultaneously and in unison:

'I'm transferring you to my manager now, sir. Please hold on to your dick.'

Then you get these buzzing and clicking noises and suddenly your line goes dead. You've been cut off. And, when you ring back, you get the same girl but this time she calls herself Natalie, even though you know her name's really Tracy. It's hopeless. In the end you give up. You didn't really want to invest your money there anyway. So you leave it where it is in the bank, so they can charge you for looking after it.

Neat, eh!

NINE

LEGGING THE DUDLEY TUNNEL

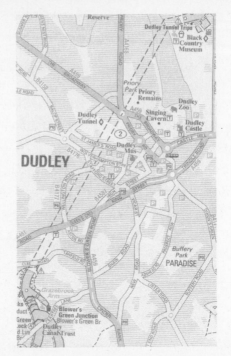

Just after this sparkling and new site of the Merry Hell complex, we were suddenly back in the familiar surroundings of old industry and the rubbish-filled cut. The contrast between the new world of Merry Hell and the old world was startling, so much so that I went into a deep shock for the next twenty minutes and noticed nothing. However, as we approached Blowers Green Pumphouse, the home of the Dudley Canal Trust, through a series of bridges including a huge railway viaduct, and came more visibly into view, a smattering of light applause turned into a great crescendo of cheering as our fellow tunnellers espied us.

Actually, that's another lie. Once again, we were too early and the only person waiting for us was Big Ron, a fellow-Thespian, who was to be our invaluable back-up for the next four days. My earlier hopes of filling the forty-seater narrowboat had already fallen victim to Mother's Day, the Grand Slam rugby international and the F.A.Cup semi-final. I had only managed to sell twenty tickets to various friends and family and luvvies, although I was delighted that Philip and Mary, two of the Bridgnorth Access group for whom we were doing this walk, had also managed to find the site, despite the fact that Philip is completely unsighted and Mary partially so!

And now, the rest of our party had, it turned out, been unable to get into the car park at the far end of the tunnel. My military-style arrangements for cars to be at both ends had foundered badly. In fact, one of the luvvies got so miffed at the poor arrangements that he flounced off home. If you can flounce off in a Lada, that is. So, although finally everyone did appear, most cars were at this Blowers Green Pumphouse end – a fact that was going to bring me trouble later.

As our bedraggled crew gathered, John and I posed with Mary and Philip, plus Philip's guide-dog Heather, for the *Express & Star* photographer who assured us that the picture would be in the following day's newspaper.

Eventually, we all managed to get aboard the Dudley Canal Trust's electric narrowboat, where Bob, our skipper for the trip, took great delight in telling us about the chains along the walls of the tunnel which we could use if the boat sank! It was only when he told us that the water was only four feet deep that we realised the unlikeliness of having to use this means of escape.

It was mid-afternoon as we entered the cavernous gloom of the Dudley Tunnel and, as my wife ministered to everyone's needs with plastic glasses of Chateau Cheap 'n' Nasty, Cap'n Bob regaled us with the story of the tunnel. It opened in 1792, at the behest as we have seen of the mighty Earl of Dudley. At the time of its opening, it was the longest tunnel in the United Kingdom and it is still the longest canal tunnel in Britain still open. It measures 3154 yards, which I suppose will now have to be written as 2900 metres because of recent Eurocrap legislation which has already forced the Black Country Museum to stop serving old-fashioned bags of sweets in ounces. During its busiest period in the middle of the nineteenth century, the Dudley Tunnel had forty thousand boats a year going through it. This was despite the fact that there could be up to three days' wait in order to enter it and that the journey could take four hours to complete.

And why did it take so long to get through? Remember that the first cut in Britain had only been built some thirty or so years beforehand and this was one of the very first canal tunnels in the world to be built. It is a remarkable piece of engineering for its time and it remains so today. Without sophisticated computational fluid dynamics techniques to hide behind, those old engineers knew their stuff, for the Dudley Tunnel was in use by working boats until 1950. However, because the tunnel is very narrow and has no towpath, the horses that towed the barges had to be walked over the hill to await the boats at the opposite end, while the boats had to be "legged" by the bargees through its length. There were even professional "leggers" that could be hired for the trip; the last of these "leggers" retired as recently as 1949.

Now, "legging" might be described as a rather sophisticated form of love-making, since it requires two people to lie on a plank back to back with their heads cradled on each other's shoulders while their feet walk along the tunnel walls, thus propelling the boat slowly through the water. The most successful "legging" is when the couple performing do so in complete harmony with each other. It is surprising what speed the boat can reach in such felicitous circumstances.

Sad to report, John claimed that an old war wound gave him backache and thus prevented him from lying down for this operation. So I was assisted in turn by other more youthful members of our merry crew as the boat eased its way through the limestone-walled tunnel like a knife through butter. I can just about remember Cap'n Bob telling us that the old-time "leggers" used to go into a trance-like state as they walked the walls. The next thing I knew we popped out of the other end of the tunnel two hours later into a canal basin with other tunnels leading off it.

As I shook myself back to life, Cap'n Bob, our fearless leader, manoeuvred the boat expertly around and into one of these tunnels which is part of the tour of the limestone caverns which goes from the Black Country Museum wharf. Part of this trip involves an audio-visual display inside one of the huge caverns created by the Earl of Dudley's miners when they extracted limestone from underground. I have to say that, when this display began with a succession of slides about the creation of the universe (Big Bang Theory, of course, not à la Bible), I could feel myself cringing as I waited for what I thought would be the inevitable, and inevitably tacky, announcement:

"And then there was Dudley!"

But I was wrong. I don't know how it was done but suddenly and amazingly we were transported visually and sonically from molten rock to the centre of the universe. I'm sorry, that should read "to the centre of the Black Country". It's a remarkably clever piece of presentation and, when you are taken on in the boat to another huge opening, known as the Singing Cavern, you are no longer surprised to learn that the Earl of Dudley had concerts in there, with full orchestras and the works. In a nearby cavern in the nineteenth century Sir Roderick Murchison addressed an estimated 15,000 members of the British Association by candlelight, for which he was acclaimed "King of Siluria". A party of these British Association members had travelled there by canal boat, the boat's cargo being described as "philosophers". I'd like to think they were the likes of Confucius, Socrates, Descartes, and Hobbes. I expect the reality was more mundane.

And then we were at the end of our underground trip, embarking carefully on to the slippery Tipton Wharf and saying farewell to Cap'n Bob and to all those who had accompanied us on our trip beneath Dudley. As we climbed up some steps to the car park, we were passed by three anxious firefighters, fully kitted out, who asked in true Monty Python fashion:

'Have you seen an 'oss in the cut?'

There's no answer to that, of course, but John, to be on the safe side, said we hadn't and they rushed off elsewhere to look for drowning 'osses.

The heavens suddenly opened as we waited in the car park for the over-complex ferrying operations to conclude, so John and I set off further down the towpath to find our overnight accommodation at the Red Lion Guesthouse in Tipton. There we were greeted by our landlady Rita who showed us our rooms and explained about the breakfast arrangements for the following morning.

'We'm doing a breakfast party 'ere at 'alf past noine,' she said, 'so yow'll have to come to the caff for yourn. It's ownly jus' across the rowd and past the soide of the cherch. Is that orlroight?'

If she was having a breakfast party at the guesthouse, why weren't we invited to have our breakfast there as well? I wondered. So I asked.

'Cos it's loike a party,' Rita explained, speaking slowly as if she was stating the bleeding obvious.

'Who for?' John asked. I could tell he was just as puzzled and moreover ready for an argument.

'Just some of the cahncil waerkers,' she said. 'They'm gooing to Uttoxeter, to the raerces, tomorrer. We allus do 'em a breakfast fust. And they'll need all the spaerce.'

Outside it was pouring down with rain now and the thought of a day out involving a breakfast party and a trip to Uttoxeter ('osses again – was this becoming a theme?) was just too overwhelming for us. Why would anyone in their right mind want to do that? It was totally baffling. But we were soaking wet so we accepted Rita's scheme, thanked her and headed off to our rooms to wash and change into drier clothing, in preparation for the evening's entertainment.

Now it is at this point that the major trauma of the day occurred. In the stupidly-complicated transportation arrangements, my good lady wife had lost her handbag with mobile phone, purse, and house keys in it. And, as John and I exited the Red Lion to find somewhere to eat, she appeared in a very distraught state. She had been driving around the area looking for us without the aid of the local A-Z, which, of course, I had with me. She feared that the most likely site of the missing handbag was the bottom of the cut but I, ever the optimist, thought it more probable that she had left it in the car of a friend of ours, a poet called Steve Clarke, who had also been on the journey through the Dudley Tunnel. Her problem was that, even if she accepted this possibility, she did not have his address or telephone number. Who did?

I did, of course.

Well, a quick telephone call to Steve established that he did indeed have the offending article and had in fact been driving around looking for my wife.

The plan had been for John and me to eat at a pub called The Pie

Factory in Tipton, so we agreed to meet Steve in the car park there. If I say that the atmosphere was tense for that twenty minutes, does that convey the mood sufficiently? I think not. Steve's subsequent arrival and return of the missing handbag did little or nothing to alleviate matters. He and John went into The Pie Factory for a drink while my wife and I had a friendly discussion on the topic.

By the time she had driven off and I had rejoined the others in the pub, The Pie Factory had stopped serving pies. Or anything else, for that matter.

It was Sunday night. In Tipton. In the Black Country. And it was teeming down with rain. 'It wor stopping to come,' in the words of some Black Country wag I once knew.

It appeared that the only place locally serving food on a Sunday evening was nearly a mile away at a pub called – it had to be, didn't it? – The 'Ungry 'Oss. And were we glad that Steve offered to drive us there? Forget the independence! Forget the walking! We were hungry and brassed off and we could get very wet again, so we leapt into his car before he could change his mind.

As we went into The 'Ungry 'Oss, we wondered whether we'd made the right decision. Maybe a couple of bags of crisps would have been better. Maybe we should have brought sandwiches with us. Or maybe even a primus stove, a frying pan and some bacon and eggs. But it was too late. We were in and at the counter being asked for our order before we could blink.

The 'Ungry 'Oss was like the canteen at a Butlin's Holiday Camp. It was choc-a-bloc with families celebrating Mother's Day. And why were they here rather than eating out at some more salubrious establishment – a Beefeater Inn or a McDonald's, for instance? Because the portions at The 'Ungry 'Oss are gargantuan, that's why. The basic menu is limited, largely consisting of steaks, burgers or chicken, but you then get a huge mound of chips together with soggy portions of peas and carrots. The seventeen-inch Big Plate Specials start at £5.99 ("Heap Big Plate of Food!" runs the legend on the menu). It's almost tasteless but it filled a gap and that was what we needed. We had the added pleasure of a large-screen (and large-volume) TV showing a riveting football match between Kilmarnock and Celtic. What could be better?

Steve stayed with us and had a pint while we ate so I persuaded him to drive us to Dudley for a quick early evening tour. The weather was so awful by now that I just couldn't contemplate asking John to walk there, willing though I was, naturally, to maintain our original stated intentions. So, we let the car take the strain as we drove the short distance to the bus station in the centre of Dudley.

TEN

THE CURSE OF DUDLEY

Dudley is supposedly named after a Saxon lord called Dudda who staked his claim to this bit of land way back when. Personally, I have my doubts about this because, if you listen to how local people pronounce the name of their town, you'd know that they say "Duglay". Which suggests to me that this Dudda was actually called Doug!

Anyway, the first thing you see from Dudley bus station, where Steve had parked his car, is Dudley (or Duglay) Castle. Or, at least, the shell of it that remains.

'Are you ready for a bit of Kings and Queens history?' I asked John.

'I suppose so,' he answered wearily. He could see that there was no stopping me and also that Steve had wandered off as soon as I mentioned kings and queens.

'Okay, then,' I began. 'Pin back your earholes and I'll tell you.'

I pointed at the looming structure that dominates the skyline, even in the gloomy rain we were experiencing.

They say there was a Saxon castle on this site but what we were looking at was begun in 1066 by William Fitz Ansculf, one of William the Conqueror's men. Castle Hill, as it's now called, is an obvious site for a castle. If you've a penchant for castle building, you'd build one on the top of this hill, just as Fitz Ansculf did. From the top you can see all along the ridge north up towards the outskirts of Wolverhampton while to the east Birmingham is visible, though of course at the time these places hardly existed. And, of course, that just happened to be much of the land that William the Conqueror gave to his loyal supporter Fitz.

But then came the Curse of Dudley, which affected so many of Fitz Ansculf's successors. First of all there was Gervase Paganel who backed the wrong side in Prince Henry's ill-fated rebellion against his father in 1173. As his reward, Dudley castle - gate, screens, towers and banqueting hall - was knocked down and left as a ruin.

People have been knocking bits of Dudley down ever since.

Nearly one hundred years later, in 1265, the new lord, Roger de Somery, set about the rebuilding of Dudley Castle. After the de Somerys the title passed to the de Suttons who for some reason began to use the name Dudley and who oversaw further developments of the buildings. There was further rebuilding, much of it on a grand scale, in the Tudor period, initiated by a later member of this family, John Dudley, who was the Mandelson-style fixer of his time.

After Henry VIII died, this John Dudley became the most powerful man in the land, because the new monarch Edward VI was a child. To secure his power, Dudley married his son Guilford off to Lady Jane Grey and convinced Edward to make her his successor. On Edward's death in 1553, Queen Jane duly succeeded to the throne but the Curse of Dudley struck again. She had only been queen for nine days, when Mary Tudor's army marched on London and reclaimed the throne for Mary. John Dudley's reward was to be executed for treason at the Tower of London.

Forty years later the de Sutton or Sutton line died out and Dudley Castle became the property of a merchant family called Ward, who became - and remain - the Earls of Dudley. It was an illegitimate son of this gang who laid claim to the discovery of a way of smelting iron with coal. Dud Dudley (or Doug Duglay) was ordered back from his studies in Oxford to take charge of his father's ironworks in the Pensnett area. There, so he claimed, he discovered how to smelt iron but he kept the somewhat uneducated and not being aware of the fact that this particular fossil was one of the rarest of its kind in the world, he placed an advertisement in the following evening's local paper, the *Express & Star*, declaring "Old fossil for sale - best offer". He was apparently very surprised when the police appeared on his doorstep that same evening! Thereafter he was known as The Dudley Bugger.

Another Dudley bugger was James Whale, the producer of those two Hollywood horror classics of the nineteen thirties, *Frankenstein* and *The Bride of Frankenstein.* The later stages of Whale's life were portrayed in a 1999 film, *Gods and Monsters*, in which Ian McKellen played the eponymous Whale as a louche, elderly, homosexual predator.

Whale's story is an interesting one, which shows that even from the most deprived of beginnings startling careers can be built. Born 1889 in Kates Hill, Dudley, and educated at local schools, James Whale worked briefly as a cobbler but enrolled as an evening art student at Dudley School of Arts and Crafts. Captured by the Germans in World War I, he spent his time in a prison camp drawing, winning money at bridge, and indulging in amateur dramatics. After the war he joined Barry Jackson's Birmingham Repertory Company, then moved to London and was invited to produce *Journey's End* for its première, which proved to be the theatrical event of 1928. He then went to Hollywood and worked for Universal Studios, making twenty-one films over eleven years including *Showboat* with Paul Robeson and *The Invisible Man,* as well as the two horror movies already mentioned. When he was forced to retire in 1941 he took up painting but, as he grew older, he suffered several minor strokes and eventually committed suicide in 1957 at the age of sixty-eight by throwing himself into his swimming pool, fully dressed in his favourite suit and tie.

John, being a theatrical, knew all this of course. Or more likely side. Two years later, at the age of eighteen, he was picked for England at left half against Scotland - England's youngest ever player. During the remaining three years of his life, Edwards won seventeen more England caps, two League Championship medals and a losers' medal in the 1957 Cup Final.

Edwards is buried in a cemetery in Dudley. This week, as usual, a fresh bunch of red and white carnations fills the black granite vase below the headstone on his grave. The other granite vase is in the shape of a football. A red United replica shirt, brand new, has also been left there. According to the crematorium manager, visitors come to the grave all through the year, not only individuals but whole parties, as if on a pilgrimage. Not far from the cemetery is St. Francis's Church where, above the font, a stained glass window is dedicated to Edwards. It shows the athletic manchild in football kit, genuflecting, with a scrolled caption saying "God Is With Us For Our Captain."

The statue of Duncan Edwards, sculpted by the same person who had previously created the statue to Billy Wright that is sited outside Molineux Stadium in Wolverhampton, was erected in Dudley market place last year.

'Ironic, isn't it?' I said to John and Steve, as we stood beside this bronze statue that evening. 'Duncan Edwards will always be remembered like that, as a young man. If he'd lived, he'd be what? About the same age as us now? Maybe older?'

'An old man, you mean?' John replied. 'Age shall not weary and all that.'

Last year John co-wrote and directed a musical play entitled *United* for our Theatre-on-the-Steps. It took as its starting point the Munich disaster and ended with the treble-winning team of 1999. It was a deeply moving but at the same time energising show.

Yes, we can be moved. And standing by this statue in the rain that evening brought us all a sense of our own mortality.

There is another statue at the opposite end of Dudley, under the shadow of the castle. It's a statue to the Earl of Dudley, erected in 1888 and bearing the legend on its plinth that it was financed by public subscription to thank the good Earl for all his services to the people of Dudley.

'That has to be the final irony,' I said as the three of us gazed at this statue while the rain ran down our faces. 'Getting the people of Dudley to pay for a statue to commemorate the biggest family of exploitative thieves in the Black Country!'

But the night was setting in and Steve understandably wanted to get home. We didn't have time to visit Dudley Zoo in the grounds of the castle, which opened in 1937 and still attracts thousands of visitors to see the poor, mangy animals that are kept in captivity for people's entertainment and curiosity. Apparently twenty three million visitors have spent a day at the zoo in the past sixty years. And this is despite the fact that the zoo has recently been voted one of the worst in the country by some group of wildlife-anoraks with a name like People Who Love Furry Beasts *and* by Which magazine. And *they* ought to know, oughtn't they? There's a new attraction called the Bostin' Wench helium balloon, which takes people on trips five hundred feet into the air. Why? I really don't know but I'm glad we didn't have the time to find out - zoos are places I wouldn't even let my cat into!

We were even gladder to accept Steve's offer to take us back to the Red Lion Guest House, where we slid off to our bedrooms to watch *Lusty Lovelies of the Lost City*, that evening's special pay-as-you-watch adult movie.

As if!

TWELVE

SLASHING THROUGH TIPTON

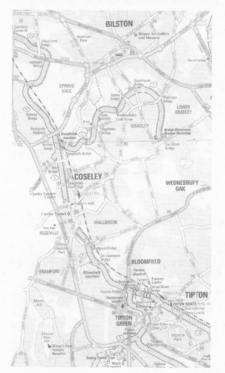

The weather forecast was right – it was snowing, as we beat our way through the slushy wilds of Tipton to the caff, which is officially known as Perry's Café for reasons that you will discover shortly.

As we flapped snow off our heads and doffed our cagoules, we were greeted very cordially by our landlady Rita, doubling up as head waitress this morning. The caff was already busy with a number of council workmen in creased, paint-stained overalls, all checking the movement of their stocks and shares in *The Mirror*. Rita steered us to a table set for two, took our order for "The Works" and then insisted on introducing us to one of the workmen sitting at an adjacent table because, she said, he too was a walker. It turned out that he'd done a twenty-mile hike in the Snowdon range the previous day and, when we told him of our five-day cut walk averaging ten miles a day, I'm pretty sure he wasn't that impressed with what we were doing. To be honest, *I* wasn't that impressed with what we were doing after listening to him!

But there was something else on Rita's mind as she brought us coffee and toast – something which she had obviously shared with the other inmates of the caff who, judging by the commentary, were regulars. The quizzical look on her face as she bustled around the room made it clear she was desperate to say something to us. Eventually she plucked up the courage.

'Did yow used to be fairmus?' she asked.

I looked up but it wasn't me her remark was addressed to. It was John, who has one of the more recognisable visages in the world. He grinned but said nothing.

'Showaddywaddy!' called out one of the workmen from his plate of fried food.

That was when we realised they were all in on it. Rita had obviously alerted them to our presence beforehand.

Just then she herself arrived with our breakfasts – steaming plates of heart-clogging cholesterol in the shape of bacon rashers, sausages, fried bread, baked beans, tomatoes and fried eggs. We looked at it, thought about being selective to protect our bodily systems, then attacked it with gusto.

Rita meanwhile had gone back to the kitchen to fetch us more toast and more coffee. When she returned, she stood by us, hands on hips, and tried again:

'Did yow do *Lily the Pink*?' she quizzed.

John grinned again and confessed all.

'Yow owes me a pint!' came a shout from the other end of the caff, which was when we appreciated the considerable debate that had preceded our arrival.

To be fair, once curiosity was satisfied, that was the end of it all. No one came pestering for autographs (neither John's nor mine!), no one asked him to give them a song, no one wanted to pass on a joke, as I've read happens to other people who have carved out a career in comedy. We were left in peace to finish our breakfasts.

It wasn't long before we were back on the towpath, our bills paid, our bags safely stored in the caff and awaiting Big Ron, our cagoules and trousers already whitened by the incessant sleet as we paused to gaze at the statue of William Perry in the Coronation Gardens park opposite the towpath.

William Perry was bareknuckle boxing champion of England from 1850 to 1857. He is better known locally as "The Tipton Slasher", allegedly because of the peculiar downward-striking blow which he inflicted on his opponents. It is worth pointing out, however, that many bareknuckle boxers of the period were reputed to strengthen their hands by soaking them overnight in vinegar; others used a cheaper substance - urine, which may be another explanation for Perry's nickname!

However, his story is a fascinating one and tells much about the Black Country itself.

Barefist fighting was a sport of the early and mid-nineteenth century, long before the Marquess of Queensberry invented the rules that have brought us a sport with such paragons of pugilistic virtue as the ear-nibbling Mike Tyson. At least there was no pretence in the nineteenth century. Barefist boxing was a bloody and brutal sport, in keeping with a bloody and brutal time with many well known fighters, with such fanciful-sounding names, as The Deaf 'Un, Bishop Smart, The Bold Smuggler, The Great Gun of Windsor, The Star of the East, and The Game Chicken.

The Tipton Slasher was brought up in Tipton but worked in London as a navvy from the age of sixteen and started boxing for money. He returned later in life to Tipton where he fought for the unofficial World Championship against the seven-foot tall black American, Charles Freeman, who was being promoted as the Champion of the World. The two boxers fought seventy rounds one afternoon in December 1842 before dark. When there was still no result, they resumed one week later and in the thirty-eighth round of that second day William Perry fell to the floor and was declared beaten.

Eat your heart out, Mohammed Ali!

But he lived to fight another day. Two more successful bouts entitled Perry to challenge the legendary Bendigo from Nottingham to a fight for the title of Champion of England. Bendigo refused to fight, so William Perry claimed the title and held it for seven years.

The Tipton Slasher lived and trained in The Fountain public house which is up the road from Perry's Café and by the side of the cut. Fortunately, it was early in the day and the pub was shut so we were not tempted in to sample its wares, not even for research purposes. But from there we could see the signs of the changes that have occurred in Tipton since the 1980s. Like so much of the Black Country, Tipton has seen prosperity turn to dereliction and decay. However, in recent years, there have been millions of pounds spent on regenerating the area. Old factories and contaminated land have been replaced with new, modern industrial parks, and surrounding landscaping. New roads have been built to give better access from the new industrial areas to the national motorway network.

Is Tipton any better off?

Not according to Rita, who laments the days when the main street was full of shops and local people could get everything they needed locally. She says the new shopping centre is a disaster because the rents are too high and half of the shops are empty. She approves of the new old people's home but thinks that there's nowhere for the old folk to go to now all the shops have closed down. Mind you, she does appreciate the fact that the cut has been cleaned up. And I was going to return to my narrative here, when I remembered another Tipton hero - Steve Bull or Bully as he's better known to thousands of Wolves fans.

Bully's story is one of those bizarre tales that turn up now and again in sport. He was signed by Wolves from his first club, the enemy West Bromwich Albion, because the latter's then manager didn't think he would ever score goals. In the next ten years he scored over three hundred goals for the Wolves and became an England international, even though he wasn't playing in the top division. He has regularly turned down transfers to other bigger clubs, because he feels at one with the supporters. He even has the unofficial Wolves fanzine named after him - *A Load of Bull*.

Bully has only recently retired from playing football but was still an important part of the Wolves set-up at the time of our walk and we managed to persuade him to join us for a photo-shoot on the canalside in Wolverhampton the week before we set out in order to help publicise the walk.

'Owamyow, orlroight?' he said to each of us, shaking our hands in turn when we met.

I ought to explain that Bully speaks pure Black Country. He may have travelled the world as a footballer of considerable status but he has never lost those dulcet Tipton tones. A television commentator once cruelly suggested that he should have an interpreter with him when he was being interviewed. Which reminds me of the time when Bill Bryson, the American travel-writer who lived for a long time in England, was asked by a man with the plummiest of plummy public school voices which accent he, Bill, had found most difficult to understand on his travels in the UK.

'What did he say?' came Bryson's brilliant put-down by way of reply, which of course had his audience hooting with merriment.

So, I wasn't going to knock Bully's accent, though I did have to help John to an understanding. However, there was something I wanted Bully's help with. You see, I had heard often over the years reference made to something called "The Lost City" in Tipton and I'd never found out where it was. So I asked Bully and he told me it was a council estate in Tipton that had only one road into it and no other way out. That was why it had been christened "The Lost City".

Unfortunately, I forgot to ask him precisely where it is so, as far as I'm concerned, it's still lost! Meanwhile, we had to turn back along the towpath.

We left The Fountain behind us and headed past a series of attractive three-storey town houses recently built abutting the cut. This was the first, but by no means the last, of such developments we were to see. They have begun to spring up along the Black Country cuts as old warehouses and factories have been cleared and the cuts themselves have been emptied of their detritus. With their high windows, paved towpaths and sometimes little balconies, these houses have the benefit of the changing light dancing on the cut surface and the peacefulness that water always instils in even the most restless of hearts.

Of course, that's just so much romantic twaddle when you're facing into the jaws of a fierce sleet storm, as we were that early morning. Cagoules zipped up tight, hoods battened around our ears, waterproof trousers squishing together, we ploughed bravely along our route. It was not unlike being on Scott's Antarctic Expedition.

'Are you sure you're happy to do this?' I queried, for probably the tenth time that morning.

I had been getting worried about John. After all, this walk was my idea. It was me that was going to write the book. John was there because .....well, because he had agreed to accompany me and because ...... it's really hard to understand other people's motivation. Many people thought I was mad to undertake this trek, so what did that make John?

Whatever he might be, he was still with me as we passed the backs of industrial units and occasionally were passed by trains on the parallel-running railway line, part of the main West Coast Line now controlled by that man in the woolly jumper, Richard Virgin. Going out of Tipton, the railway crosses the main road via a bridge. Sandwell Council has chosen to brighten people's lives with amusing decoration on several bridges. This particular one features large musical notes which are the opening bars of *Chattanooga Choo Choo* – but how would you know that unless you read it here?

To keep our spirits up in the dreadful weather, we held philosophical discussions about the long-term economic, social and cultural planning of the United Kingdom, comparing it with the superior planning John had witnessed in France, where he had lived for several years. In the space of three-quarters of an hour we had solved most of Britain's problems and, carried away by the stimulation of the discussion, we had forgotten the cold, we had forgotten the sleet, and we had almost forgotten the cut.

Then suddenly we were in the Coseley Tunnel – one of the significant improvements brought about by Thomas Telford when he chopped so many miles off the cut between Wolverhampton and Birmingham. The Coseley Tunnel is 327 metres long and there is a towpath along one side of it, guarded by black-painted railings. We became aware of an odd sensation as we walked through because, although we could see the end of the tunnel ahead of us, our sense of distance was so distorted that we fell into a kind of trance as we walked so that we could not see the railings beside us. At the far end, the reflection of the curved roof of the tunnel in the water below gave the curious illusion that we were walking in a tube.

And then, suddenly, we were out. Out into the snow and sleet and grim greyness of the morning. Out to see the first Black Country 'osses of our journey.

There are hundreds of 'osses in the Black Country. Or should I say 'undreds of 'osses? They tend to be strong, sturdy-looking animals, usually of mixed parentage and mixed colour scheme. They graze on patches of grass wherever these can be found, frequently in the middle of heavily-industrialised areas. No one knows who owns them but many of them are at the end of a single chain, fastened into the ground, so someone certainly does own them. Some people say it's gipsies. Some say it's rag-and-bone men. Others say it's the ghosts of long-dead pitmen who tend the horses. But no one really knows.

There's nothing after the tunnel to tell you that this is Coseley you are passing through but, since there is very little memorable about Coseley anyway, this is probably no bad thing. Bilston, on the other hand, which was our next port of call, promised something else.

THIRTEEN

A BILSTON DIVERSION

At the Millfields Bridge we left the towpath to walk the short distance into Bilston. Coming up on to the road we passed the entrance to Tarmac's offices, which are a reminder to me of the Big Four major works that once dominated Bilston and which were where most of the people I grew up with found themselves working in the late nineteen fifties and early nineteen sixties. The Big Four were Stewarts & Lloyds, John Thompson's, GKN Sankeys, and Tarmac. Today only the last remains and that has just been swallowed up by a giant American conglomerate. I have no idea what happened to many of my childhood companions. Some no doubt used their redundancy money to pay off their mortgages and live a life of leisure. Some would already have moved off into other places of work. Others will have tried to set themselves up in business, selling hamburgers from a Union Jack-decorated caravan in a lay-by on the new Black Country Route.

I wanted to visit Bilston because it is at the heart of the Black Country. The abundance of coal and iron ore in the area attracted industrialists from the middle of the sixteenth century onwards. By the end of the next century five thousand tons of coal a year were flowing out of the many mines in the Bilston area. By the end of the following century, this had risen to one million tons per year. The growth in employment opportunities brought large numbers of immigrants from other parts of Britain, notably from Shropshire, Scotland and Ireland, as is evidenced by street names in Bilston like Salop Street, Caledonia Road and Shamrock Yard.

In 1772 "Iron-Mad Jack" Wilkinson was seduced by the promise of endless coal and left his native Cumbria to set up shop in Bradley, Bilston. He built the world's first steam-powered blast furnace, using coke instead of coal to smelt the iron. "The mother furnace" of the whole of the Black Country iron industry was a significant factor in the growth of the Industrial Revolution and put Bilston well and truly on the map. The greater blast pressure of Wilkinson's works enabled him to manufacture strong, accurate cylinders which James Watt took full advantage of in the development of his steam engine. His factory also made cast iron cannon for use in the American War of Independence and there are tales of Wilkinson suppling cannon to Napoleon - capitalism has always had a strong patriotic flavour! Among the unusual accomplishments of Wilkinson's ironworks was the building of the first iron boat, a brigantine called *The Trial*, which, when launched in 1787, disappointed a huge crowd who had turned up expecting it to sink.

Wilkinson paid his workers in coins which he minted himself, with his own portrait on. Needless to say, these could only be spent at the shops which Wilkinson himself owned. It's no surprise that he grew very rich and lived to be eighty years old, which was twice the average life-span of his workers. He kept two iron coffins in his house and he was reputedly buried in one of them. However, there is some dispute as to where this burial took place, since it is alleged that the heavy iron coffin was dropped in Morecambe Bay as the pall-bearers got caught short by the incoming tide.

Bilston went from strength to strength. The invention of a converter by Henry Bessemer in the mid-nineteen hundreds allowed iron to be turned cheaply into steel. This led directly to the building of the Springvale Steelworks in Bilston by Alfred Hickman in the eighteen eighties and it was this factory that subsequently became Stewarts & Lloyds and later, under nationalisation, British Steel. Its most famous symbol was the "Elisabeth" blast furnace, which was named after the daughter of the chairman of Stewarts & Lloyds who officiated at the blowing in and christening ceremony. "Elisabeth", or "Big Bessie" as she was affectionately known (the furnace, not the daughter!), began operating at Bilston Steelworks in 1954 and produced over five million tonnes of pig iron in its lifetime. However, in 1979 Bilston Steelworks closed because of the international recession and one year later "Big Bessie" was demolished.

All of this we learned from a splendid little display, clearly marked and easy to follow, in Bilston Library on the traffic-filled Mount Pleasant - and when was that last a pleasant view? - at the far end of town from where we entered from the canalside. When we got there, our bad luck looked set to continue for it was closed. However, generous-hearted members of the library staff opened it up especially for us. Unfortunately, there is no descriptive literature available so I had to scribble all these juicy titbits down from the displays as we walked through.

There is also a very attractive display of Bilston enamels in the library, though once again there are no leaflets available for visitors to take away. This enamel-ware was fashionable in the latter half of the eighteenth century and much of it was made in Bilston. It consisted largely of small metal boxes, finely decorated with an enamelled surface. These beautiful miniature boxes were designed to carry such things as scents, scissors, beauty patches or bon-bons to perfume the breath in the days before dental hygiene. Snuff boxes were perhaps the most common of these miniatures and it is incredible to realise how prevalent snuff-taking was at the time in all classes of society. There were actually schools which taught the do's and dont's of offering and taking snuff. Imagine the outcry if similar schools were created today for coke-snorting techniques and ecstasy-management!

Changes of fashion accounted for the decline of the enamel trade in the early part of the nineteenth century but it was the closure of the steelworks that marked the end of heavy industry in Bilston and led to the changes which are still taking place in the way that Bilston sees itself. It had already lost much of its separate identity by the time it was brought under the Wolverhampton umbrella in the local government reorganisation of 1966 but now, since the opening of the Black Country Route sweeping around the south of the town, Bilston is being reinvented once again.

Much of the town is now pedestrianised with some attractive street art in the form of ornate cast iron seating and sculptures, although there are a lot of empty shops. The once-infamous Bilston Market, where it was reputed that anything and everything could be bought, has been rebuilt in a new site but still throbs with busyness. What was once The Palace cinema has now become the Imperial Palace Social Club offering various nightclub discos including, "The Vivatius Maria", and the old Drill Hall has recently become "The Robin R 'n' B Club 2". This latter features tribute bands, which are a bizarre phenomenon of the turn of the century - bands which copy in dress and sound well known acts of popular music's past. The Bootleg Beatles and the Counterfeit Stones are fairly obvious, as I suppose are Fred Zeppelin and the Electric Live Orchestra, but I had to work hard to see that Once More into the Bleach was a tribute to Blondie.

But not all has changed in Bilston. After our visit to the Library and a quick tour of Bilston Market, we headed back through the pedestrianised town, till we came to two of Bilston's most famous hostelries opposite each other near the top of High Street. The Greyhound and Punchbowl is reputedly the former Stow Heath Manor House. Its oldest part is a timber-framed building dating back to 1450, with a Jacobean moulded plaster ceiling and carved overmantels and panelling (in case you're an architecture-anorak). But it was the public house opposite which was our intended lunchtime destination. The Trumpet has always been known locally as The Cunt & Trumpet, because of its reputation for putting on good quality, local jazz and for providing a showcase for the female talent of Bilston. The jazz still goes on there but I wanted to find out more about its other attractions.

Unfortunately, although it was past midday, The Trumpet was, of course, closed. So, with the weather still dreadful, we went into The Greyhound opposite hoping for some lunch. You'll have guessed, of course, by now that it wasn't serving food that day, so we were pointed towards The Swan at the top end of the town. Here at last we enjoyed pints of Banks's bitter and some cheap hot food, while drying off in the warm atmosphere.

'Are you sure you're happy to continue?' I queried, for certainly the twenty fifth time that day.

'It's up to you,' he answered but I could sense the wavering in his voice.

'We could always sneak home now and start again in the morning,' I suggested, looking at my nearly empty glass and tempted to have another pint. 'No one would know.'

But we were wrong, for just at that moment in walked Big Ron, who had just transported our bags from one guest house to another. There was no way we could admit defeat now so, suitably fortified though not entirely blissful, we strolled back toward the Millfields Bridge and the cut to resume our journey.

'You wouldn't naturally associate Bilston with cricket, would you?' I said to John nonchalantly as we resumed our trek towards Wolverhampton.

I had just remembered another fascinating facet of the place.

'You're not going to tell me that Ian Botham used to come to The Trumpet, are you?' he tried.

'Not quite,' I replied, smirking. 'But Sir Henry Newbolt came from Bilston. His father was the local vicar.'

'Not *the* Sir Henry Newbolt,' quoth John, throwing out his hands in mock surprise. 'Who's he?'

'The poet. You must have heard these lines:

There's a breathless hush in the Close tonight -
Ten to make and the match to win -
A bumping pitch and a blinding light,
An hour to play and the last man in.
And it's not for the sake of a ribboned coat,
Or the selfish hopes of a season's fame,
But his Captain's hand on his shoulder smote -
'Play up! play up! and play the game!'

'That was him?' John asked incredulously. 'Gosh!'

This was said in a tone I can only describe as dripping in post-modern irony, but I was not to be put off.

'*Vitaï Lampada*,' I concluded. 'One of the most moving poems of our time.'

'Sounds more like a motor scooter to me,' he answered.

And all I was trying to do was help him understand we folk from the Black Country weren't all as thick as the Thirty Foot Coal Seam!

FOURTEEN

APPROACHING WOLVES

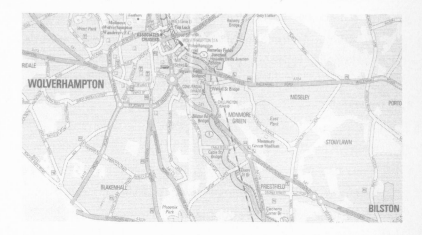

It was only two more snow-battered miles along the towpath to Wolverhampton. The cut on this stretch is surrounded on both sides by industrial units of varying sizes, most of them humming with machine noise. Virtually all of these factories are protected from the canalside by high walls topped with lethal-looking razor-wire, presumably because they have been raided by marauders from the cut in the past. One yard was piled high with containers labelled Liquid Argon.

'D'you think there's a black market in Liquid Argon?' quizzed John. 'D'you think there's dealers standing at club doorways selling Liquid Argon at fifty quid a go? What do they do with it? Mix it with their Bacardi Breezers? Down it neat? Sip it through a straw? Inject it?'

Such pleasant fantasies entertained us as we passed under the succession of bridges that lead into the Broad Street basin in the centre of Wolverhampton, our final destination for the day. We climbed gratefully up to the roadside opposite the old British Waterways depot which is now a nightclub called, curiously enough, "The Canal", voted the UK's best nightclub by somebody or other.

According to the history books, Wolverhampton was founded in 994 when Lady Wulfruna, the sister of the dead King Edgar, endowed land in Heantun that had been given to her by the new king, Ethelred the Unready. The place therefore became Wulfruna's Heantun, later corrupted to Wolverhampton.

The next significant event to happen in the town was in 1877 when a team known as St.Luke's Football Club came into being. Two years later they merged with another local team called The Wanderers, and thus was born Wolverhampton Wanderers. In 1887 the team became founder members of the Football League. This team was to become the legendary Wolves, whose exploits in gold and black have played a crucial part in the construction of my mental map of the world.

I can't remember precisely what the first football match I attended was. I would have been eight or nine years old and clutching my dad's hand. I was probably wearing a blue gabardine mackintosh, short grey trousers, a grey Viyella shirt, and a schoolboy's cap. It was almost certainly a midweek evening match because my dad worked on Saturdays. It was probably damp and the steamy breath of the crowds winding down Waterloo Road towards Molineux Stadium would have mingled with the pungent, brown factory smoke that was so prevalent in those pre-pollution control days. In my dream, the match would have been against our great rivals - the Baggies of West Bromwich - and we would have thrashed them, trashed them and trounced them 8-0! Yes, we, because already from that first match I had become part of that collective mass whose hopes and aspirations were raised or knocked down by the performance of our eleven heroes on the pitch each week.

From then on I was hooked - the orginal soccer-anorak. Though I wasn't able to go to matches regularly because of my young age and my dad's working patterns, I followed the Wolves' exploits in the newspapers, I collected cigarette cards with my heroes' photos on and I kept scrapbooks of cuttings from wherever I could find them. And, as I got older, I was able to start going to matches on my own, for in those innocent post-war days, a thirteen-year old boy could stand in a crowd of fifty thousand plus without feeling frightened of anything other than his own excitement overcoming him.

This was the golden age of Wolverhampton Wanderers. It was the age of the England half-back line of the elegant Bill Slater, the incomparable Billy Wright, and the fierce-tackling Ron Flowers. It was the age of the pocket dynamo winger Johnny Hancocks, of the ball-dribbling genius Peter Broadbent, of the goal-scoring left-footers Dennis Wilshaw and Jimmy Mullen, and of the agile green-jumpered goalkeeper Bert "the Cat" Williams. Managed by the legendary Stan Cullis, this golden team won the First Division Championship three times and the FA Cup once between 1950 and 1960. As importantly, with the introduction of floodlights Wolves led the way into Europe, inviting many of the most famous clubs from the continent to play in front of the enthralled Molineux crowds. Spartak from Russia, Honved from Hungary, Moscow Dynamo and Real Madrid all came and were beaten by the local heroes. I'd like you to believe I went to at least one of these matches but I didn't. However, I can vividly recall hearing the cheer that went up when Jimmy Mullen scored the winning goal against Moscow Dynamo, because I was cycling home from scouts and we lived four miles from Molineux. Some cheer! It filled the autumn night sky. Of course, by the time I got home the match was over and all I saw on the new TV set we had bought for the Coronation two years previously was the two teams trooping off the pitch, hot breath steaming from their mouths.

Now, if you're a woman, or from another country, or simply not interested in football, you'll be asking yourself what on earth this load of cobblers is about, won't you?

So why am I telling you all this? I suppose I'm trying to explain, to myself as much as anyone else, why football still gives me a fix and why I'm still prone to plan my life around being able to see some televised football match. Why should this be? After all, I was no great shakes at playing the game as a youngster. At junior school I was always first reserve and at The Grammar School I only managed to get into the house second team. The only time I managed to get a regular game was when I formed my own team after I came back from university. We called ourselves the Bar Stewards, which we thought was a terribly funny bowdlerization of Bastards. I picked the team, which always featured me as centre-forward; I picked the opposition, which normally had to contain at least three people in wheelchairs; I wrote the very witty programme notes; and I bought the referee two pints of Banks's Mild (Very Smooth. Very Mooreish) to make sure we won. At the end of a fabulously-successful season, we hired a coach to drive us in triumph through Wolverhampton and out to a hotel in Penkridge for a celebratory dinner.

Sad, eh?

And yet the same thing seems to have happened to large numbers of otherwise sane, educated, decent men. You know instantly what someone means when they say to you, "Did yow goo Saturday?" You know they're not talking about doing the weekly shopping at Tesco or going to a lawnmower demonstration or watching your daughter's ballet

102

class, all of which are perfectly legitimate activities for a Saturday. No, immediately you know they're asking if you went to see your local team playing football. And it doesn't matter whether you went or not, or even if they went or not, because the next ten minutes (or hours) will be spent dissecting the most recent performance of your team. Given the fact that only one team can ever win the championship in any season, this inevitably means that most of this conversation is conducted in the deepest gloom. Well, it certainly is if you're a Wolves supporter, as I have been ever since those halcyon days (soccer-anoraks always use the word 'halcyon', though they don't know what it means) back in the nineteen fifties. As I write this, at the start of the new millennium, Wolves are languishing (that's another posh word we soccer-anoraks always use when our team isn't doing very well) in seventh place in the First Division, which is what the Second Division is now called since the advent of the Premier League. Seventh place is where Wolves always finish. And that means they don't feature in the play-off matches at the end of the season that determine which team will accompany the two automatically-promoted teams, Charlton and Manchester City in this case, into the Premier League.

At least I don't have one of those cardboard cut-outs in a Wolves strip nodding away in the back window of my car!

That's enough of that. Wolverhampton is famous for a few other things as well. It was the birthplace of the famous thief Jonathan Wild, who was known as Chief Thieftaker General of Great Britain because he informed on other criminals and virtually controlled the whole of the London underworld till he was hanged at Tyburn in 1725. It was the home for a few years of Button Gwinnett, who married the daughter of a local tea-merchant and then emigrated to America, where he became governor of the state of Georgia. His name is second on the list of signatories of The Declaration of Independence and he has a little blue plaque in the middle of the town dedicated to him by the Daughters of the American Revolution, whoever they may be.

It was also the home of trolley-bus manufacturers Guy Motors, of AJS and Norton motorcycles, on which many an Isle of Man TT race was won, and of Sunbeam Motors. It was in a Sunbeam car on Daytona Beach in 1927 that Henry Seagrove became the first person to exceed 200 miles per hour, for which he was later knighted. None of these companies exist now of course, as international capitalism has found places in the Far East to manufacture such things more cheaply.

And it was the birthplace of Rachael Heyhoe Flint who was captain of the England Ladies Cricket team for ten years, who in 1999 was one of only ten women accepted as Honorary Members of the M.C.C. and who is now a Public Relations Consultant with Wolverhampton Wanderers. You see, there is no escape!

Oh yes, Wolverhampton was where the first traffic lights were trialled in 1927. Ever since then the local boy-racers have been striving to see who can jump the lights fastest.

Near one of those sets of traffic lights by the market was our lodging for the night at the inestimable New Inn. As we waited for Jackie our landlady to collect the keys to our rooms, we were confronted at the bar by a small moustachioed man clutching his pint of Banks's mild (Very Smooth. Very Mooreish).

'Scuse me axing?' he began. 'But wor yow in Scaffold?'

When John confirmed that this was in fact true, the little man thrust out his chest and simultaneously his right hand.

'Very pleased to mate yow,' he said, as if it was he who was granting John the favour.

I realised that I was going to have to endure a lot more of this.

We were glad to escape from the little man and be shown our rooms. It was a real pleasure to put on fresh clothing after the weather we had had and to know that our serious perambulations were over for the day.

I suggested to John that we set off to explore the centre of Wolverhampton and where better to begin than Beatties coffee bar, the legendary haunt of the blue-rinse and mink stole brigade? Beatties is the posh shop in town, established when the town was at the height of its prosperity, and is still the favoured establishment of the wives of garagists and other nouveaux riches of South Staffordshire. Actually, apart from two young mothers breast-feeding their babies, we were the only people in the coffee bar. But I have to tell you that those two cups of coffee, in the warm ambience of Beatties and wearing clean dry clothes, while watching the snowflakes floating thickly on to those who passed beneath us as we gazed out of the window, were the finest sustenance you could imagine.

We left Beatties via the perfume counters – those thickly-scented monuments to female vanity which form my lasting memory of entering the establishment. I was always terrified of the sophistication of those shop assistants dressed in black from head to foot, with their layers of make-up perfectly applied, their long scarlet fingernails, their stiletto heels and their fake pearls. I longed for them to offer me a whiff from their tiny perfume-sprays. I lusted after them all through my teenage years, or at least when I wasn't watching the Wolves play!

As if still that forlorn teenager, I stopped to gaze at the current crop of scent-sprayers.

'What now?' John asked, pausing with his hands on his hips and giving me one of his withering looks.

'Have you no soul?' I enquired. 'Look at them. They're still there. Just the same as they were when I was younger.'

'And I suppose they didn't look at you then any more than they're looking at you now,' John said dryly.

He can be so cruel. But he was right. It was time to exit my fantasy.

FIFTEEN

WOLVERHAMPTON IN THE DARK

Once upon a time every town centre in the land housed the major banks, usually in Victorian-style buildings. In recent years, however, these selfsame banks have realised that they can get more of our money off us by turning themselves into bars, where the young gather and get smashed on Hooch or Metz or Smirnoff Mules. Wolverhampton has followed this trend and buildings that formerly housed worthy money laundering businesses have in recent years been converted to meet the needs of the large and getting-larger student population. They have been rechristened with names like "Pepper's", "Rothwell's", "It's A Scream" and "The Dog's Bollocks". And that's not all. Wolverhampton is reputedly one of the major nightlife centres in the kingdom. What I used to know as the Savoy cinema has been rebuilt as the Atlantis nightclub and where the Hippodrome used to stand in Queen Square there is now a Yates's Wine Lodge.

Now, if you're of a certain generation reading this, you'll be a bit taken aback at finding a Yates's Wine Lodge being one of the trendier places for young people to get drunk in. You'll remember the time when they were the hang-outs for all those sad souls who wanted to keep their alcohol levels up on cheap sherry. And you'd be right because, although they began life as places where port and sherry could be sipped by the discriminating, they later degenerated into dives where alkies derived their sustenance. But there has been a relaunch. Nowadays Yates's Wine Lodges are spreading like measles across the land and they're just the same as all those other chains of trendy boozers. Shame, really. The alkies outside Yates's with their sherry bottles hidden inside brown paper bags were part of the colour of my youth.

But our first stop was not Yates's but the splendid Chubb Locks building, which has been preserved by the town council and now houses a cinema and a number of café bars. We then passed the Grand Theatre, recently refurbished at great expense but, especially for our arrival in town, closed for the night. Which was fortunate in fact because neither of us really fancied seeing ancient TV stars like Kate O'Mara and Ian Lavender in the farce *Passport to Pimlico* on later in the week, despite the advertising boards outside which pronounced it as "Hilarious". Old farce passes for high art in Wolverhampton. Later in the season the town is promised The Krankies. How much more can Wulfrunians take?

The Art Gallery was much better. Up the flight of steps and under the portico supported by six red granite columns we went into the Italianate building erected in the nineteenth century in the heyday of proud civic construction. The ground floor was home that week to an exhibition of works by an artist named Johnny White, entitled Manic Mechanics. The sculptures, huge pieces of metal engineering, included a pink cow, an exercise bike attached to a gramophone which played Max Bygraves's *Fings Ain't What they Used To Be*, a BSE Minotaur, a swinging donkey made of spoons and a giant cyclops. A gallery on the first floor contained individual pieces of art work selected by gallery staff from the vaults with their thoughts appended. A nice touch, especially as one selection was a very lovely Bilston enamel.

'Where are we going?' John asked, as I led him out of the Art Gallery after our tour.

'Molineux Stadium,' I told him.

'I thought you promised not to mention the Wolves again.'

'I did,' I countered, pressing ahead through the underpass. 'But I have to show you something.'

'Not another bloody footballer!' he said.   ᵔe Minister

'No, not just another footballer,' I said, as I paused ᵔolitical
look in the direction I was pointing. 'Probably one of the gᵔ
footballers of all time.'

We gazed together at the bronze statue of William Ambrose [Billy]
Wright, the Wolves and England captain who won over one hundred
international caps playing for his country. After his death, public
subscription raised the money for his statue which was sculpted by James
Butler R.A. It was unveiled by Joy Beverley Wright, Billy's widow and
famous in her own right as one of the singing Beverley Sisters, in front
of the stand named after him in the new Molineux as a permanent
memorial.

Two other strands of Wolverhampton came together during our
evening tour because we chose to have a pint of Banks's in The Wanderer
public house in Molineux Street near to the Wolves ground. Now Banks's,
apart from being one of the few remaining homes of the correctly-used
apostrophe, has its brewery in Wolverhampton and Banks's beers are
infamous in the area. In the last few years, thanks to a thrusting managing
director, the sleepy company has been involved in aggressive take overs
of other breweries - Cameron's and Marston's being just two such. It
has also spent heavily on marketing itself, using the clever slogan
"Unspoilt by progress", thus using sophisticated modern advertising
techniques to tug at the nostalgic heartstrings. Its latest advertising
wheeze, unveiled during the week of our journey, involves paying the
actor Roger Moore, he of James Bond and The Saint fame, large amounts
of money to pretend that he likes drinking Banks's bitter. The slogan
used to push this is "Very Smooth. Very Mooreish." It apparently cost
over a million pounds to make and, purely by coincidence, the price of
a pint of Banks's beer went up sixpence the same week.

highly-educated man in a position of great power and influence gave credence to the racist attitudes which have blighted so much of Black Country life in the past forty years. By his behaviour he gave licence to all those white people who were happy to accept the quirks of Scottish, Welsh, Irish, Polish, Jewish and Czechoslovak immigrants but not that of those whose skin was of a different colour. By his speech he gave words to the previously-silent and encouraged the torrent of abuse that flowed through the Black Country and scarred the lives of those who suffered it and equally of those who delivered it.

And he was supposed to be clever?

Now, at the start of the new millennium, Wolverhampton has a population of a quarter of a million. One fifth of those are from ethnic minority groups. Having 'the whip hand over the white man'? I think not. 'Foaming with blood'? Hardly. Nowadays, black and Asian people are to be found at all levels of all professions in the Black Country. In fact the current Chief Executive of Wolverhampton Borough Council is black. That just shows how far things have come. Good on you, Wolverhampton! You may not have the best football team any longer but you are a leading light in another way.

Another citizen of the new Wolverhampton is Mohammed, our waiter in the Bilash Tandoori Restaurant, where we finally decided to eat. The Bilash is round the back of St.Peter's Gardens slap bang in the town centre. These surround the church that has been at the heart of Wolverhampton since before Lady Wulfruna's day, a fact memorialised by the Anglo-Saxon cross shaft that stands in front of it.

I have to say that, next to the cup of coffee in Beatties, the murghi-diya-shorisha that I had in the Bilash that evening was one of the finest meals I have ever eaten. The meal itself is a Bangladeshi dish comprising chicken marinated in mustard oil, garlic and ginger then cooked in a wonderful array of spices. The Cobra beer was excellent. The service was quick, friendly and responsive. And the price was not extortionate. By the time we finished we had forgotten the rigours of the day.

After we had eaten, I led John back through Queen Square, where I felt I had to point out the statue which dominates its centre.

'That's Prince Albert, Queen Victoria's husband,' I informed John.

'Why does that matter?' demanded John, who was clearly fed up with all my anecdotal coverage of Wolverhampton.

'It doesn't,' I replied. 'But, after three pints of beer and a curry, I have this desperate need to tell you that the statue of Prince Albert was commissioned by the Widows of Wolverhampton and that Queen Victoria herself unveiled it in 1866, her first public engagement since her husband had died.'

'Really?' he said. 'And I always thought it was Billy Connolly who made her better!'

SIXTEEN

TRAPPED IN WEDNESFIELD

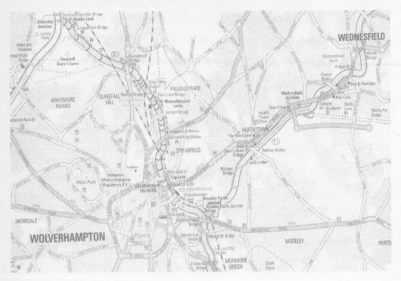

Morning came with the throbbing sound of a generator choking into life outside my window. I flipped back the curtain and, sure enough, there was a roadworks sign, there was a lorry with three workmen reading *The Sun*, and there was a generator chugging noisily and, as far as I could tell, for no reason. The good news was that it was no longer snowing. The bad news was that the previous evening's snow had settled and, even though it was only a thin dusting, it promised to make underfoot surfaces treacherous. I sat up in bed and looked round at the other three empty beds and asked myself what sort of visitors would want a room in the middle of Wolverhampton with four beds in it.

I washed and dressed and, avoiding the attentions of the rottweiler who guarded the roof of the New Inn, went down for breakfast. The bar was our breakfasting room. In one corner The Big Breakfast Show was screaming away on the television, behind me a woman was busy scrubbing the bar counter clean, and on the wall opposite me was a sign that read "GREY PEAS AND BACON £1.40". I was curious and John was still in the bath, so I decided to ask our landlady Jackie.

'Yow doh wanner know,' she replied, grimacing. 'It's vile!'

'But what is it?' I pressed. 'I've lived in the Midlands all my life and I've never heard of Grey Peas and Bacon.'

'Paes,' she corrected me. 'They'm them dried paes yow feed to pidgins.'

Her face had gone a distinct shade of grey and I could tell she was finding it increasingly difficult to speak. Whatever this delicacy was, it clearly did not cause trills of delight to Jackie's palate.

'It's vile,' she repeated, then launched into a full explanation, as if only by doing so could she drive the image out of her mind. 'I useta mek it for me 'usband. Yow 'ave to sowk the paes for two days, then you bile them up with bits of baercon and onions. They love it rahnd 'ere. Some on 'em'll come in 'ere every day and 'ave it. I suppose it's warm and it's filling. But I cor touch it. It's vile.'

So that was that then. I could tell from the look of distaste on her face that she wasn't going to tell me any more and, since John still hadn't arrived, I decided to seek the answer to another of the mysteries of the New Inn.

'The room I was in last night......' I began.

'Was yow warm enough?' she interrupted, clearly anxious. 'Ownly I thought about yow when I was going 'ome in the snow last noight.'

'Yes, yes,' I assured her. 'I was fine. But I was wondering who your usual customers are who want four beds in the same room.'

'Chaps doing werk in the town, y'know, carpenters, electricians, that sort of thing,' she told me, moving in the direction of the kitchen as if this was one of the daftest questions she'd ever been asked. 'They'm on contract werk and they just want somewhere cheap to kip for the noight. The only other place is The Wheatsheaf and they doh 'ave tellies in the rooms theer.'

You see, there is an explanation for everything.

'It's going to get colder,' John said, as he bounced fresh-faced into the bar. 'Have you seen the weather forecast? Minus two for most of the day.'

'Yow'll want the cooked breakfast then?' asked Jackie, grinning round the kitchen door.

Sure enough, it was very cold and there was a keen wind blowing into our faces as we left the BCN in Wolverhampton and joined the towpath alongside the Wyrley and Essington Canal (the Curly Wyrley to canal-anoraks, who have a poetic streak after all), travelling east in the direction of Walsall. To be fair, however, the wind was drying the towpath quickly and, although there were some traces of snow left from the previous night, it very soon disappeared.

The journey took us initially under the main railway lines just outside Wolverhampton station, then through the same sort of industrial area that we had encountered on entering the town the day before. Sooner than I expected, however, we came to a place of stark contrasts - New Cross Bridge at the edge of Wolverhampton. The bridge itself is very old, with its blue brick base recently added to with newer red bricks. Trees and shrubs sweep down to the water on one side while a newly-laid path on the towpath side takes you up on to the apex of the bridge. And it is there that the contrast is so apparent.

To the left stands that giant honeycomb called New Cross Hospital which was originally built as a workhouse for five hundred inmates, became a hospital in 1909 and now is the major hospital for the Wolverhampton district. This is the place where, if my doctor's prognosis has any substance, I shall probably end up having my left knee replaced in twenty years' time, so I'd better be careful what I write here. After all, I don't want some Hattie Jacques-type matron quoting my words back at me and threatening to withdraw my Lucozade allowance, or some Kenneth Williams-type surgeon trying to replace my knee-joint with something manufactured from a warthog's backside in the name of scientific research.

So, let me focus on the facts. Last year the hospital had an income of £105.36 million; it employed 3075.69 people (and you'll have to work out the point 69 – I couldn't possibly comment, given my anxieties for the future). In the course of the year, it treated 77,797 inpatients, 296,208 outpatients and 118,226 accident and emergency cases. That makes a grand total of almost half a million people receiving the equivalent of about £200 worth of treatment each. And that includes doctors, nurses, ancillary staff, and the costs of whatever treatment is necessary. That doesn't seem to me to be a bad deal. In fact, it's a damn good deal and it's the reason why the National Health Service, despite its constant critics, is still the envy of the world.

So go gentle on my knee, guys, okay?

On the right hand side of the New Cross Bridge, on a site where the Bentley Canal used to be, stands that wonderful monument to the latter years of the twentieth century – the Leisure Complex. This one is known as Bentley Bridge Leisure and houses a Cineworld cinema with fourteen screens (the week's attractions included Oscar-winners *American Beauty* and *The Cider House Rules* as well as the Bollywood epics *Hera Phiri* and *Dulhan Hum Le Jayenge*). It also boasts four American fast food outlets in Pizza Hut, KFC, Macdonald's and Fatty Arbuckle's. Another major development on this Leisure site is the amazing Healthland, which is a huge keep-fit enterprise with all the up-to-date, fat-burning, muscle-building, cardiovascular-enhancing gear. Healthland has been designed with giant see-through windows so that you can watch all these trendy people in their purple and pink lycra leotards with sweatbands on their wrists and foreheads as they pound the treadmills or rotate the exercise-bike pedals or pump the weights. The ironic result is that it has now become a favourite sport in Wolverhampton to stand outside these windows teasing those inside by waving your burger and fries or four-cheese pizza at them.

Away from all this excitement and by the side of the cut, where a very brief stretch of the old Bentley Canal has been preserved, presumably to encourage leisure-craft to moor alongside as they go for their pizzas or burgers to wave at the Healthland masochists, is a new pub. It is called the Nickelodeon and is one of the Tom Cobleigh chain of pubs which Rank have been erecting around the country. A motto under its name states: "Unspoilt pub for nice people". This is to distinguish it from all the other pubs in the area which are, by definition, "Spoilt pubs for vile people". Just so as you know.

The towpath on this stretch has been very pleasantly refurbished with concreted pathways and metal benches, so that those nice people may, if they choose, bring their drinks outside in the warm weather and smile nicely at each other, while holding nice conversations about carpets.

It was only a short distance from here to Wednesfield, a town that the Curly Wyrley winds sinuously through. Once again we ventured off the towpath to investigate the town centre, which has recently been semi-pedestrianised, as a result of the road-building scheme which was also responsible for Bentley Bridge Leisure. It's the semi in the semi-pedestrianised that is the cause of problems because a bus route has been left through the centre of the town and, despite the very clear signposting, there are still boy-racers who prefer to take this route. This we were told by a police officer we accosted outside the Holistic Therapy Centre. (Get that, all ye who sneer at Black Country folk and their ways. Holistic Therapy in Wednesfield, no less.) The policeman also told us that, since the semi-pedestrianisation, shops' takings have shown a marked upturn. Looking around we could see why, since the town is a secure place for the elderly and those with pushchairs or young children to stroll through. It also seems to be a thriving shopping centre with no vacant shops, a Post Office with an unusually-lettered sign, three butchers and three bakers, though sadly no candlestick maker.

Wednesfield used to be full of small industries making a variety of metal products, most notoriously animal traps, especially ones to capture large animals. These were exported all over the world. It was also reputed to be a place where man-traps were manufactured but there are no surviving examples, unless you count the local prostitutes. Sidebotham's trap works from Wednesfield was dismantled and rebuilt at the Black Country Museum in the early nineteen eighties, complete with its stamping, pressing and punching machines, its single-cylinder gas engine, its forge hearth and its fly presses.

There was one trap awaiting us, however. A tiger-trap. Although it was still only midway through the morning and we had quite a way to go, we were decidedly cold and took the decision to warm up with a cup of coffee. The only place we could see likely to be serving such a tipple was called The Royal Tiger, a pub which rather carelessly had failed to check with all the other closed places on our route and had decided to open on the very day that we arrived in Wednesfield. This much we gathered as we walked through the front door to be greeted by smiling barmaids in smart outfits and smiling brewery representatives overseeing their new venture. We ordered our coffees and explored the place as we sipped.

The Royal Tiger is one of the J.D.Wetherspoon chain of pubs, which "specialise in the sale of cask-conditioned beers from Britain's regional brewers" and "with the absence of music and pool tables appeal, in particular, to a more mature clientèle and to women". It was certainly a more mature clientèle in The Royal Tiger that morning, since every old cap in the district had been drawn in by the promise of Banks's beer at less than £1 a pint. Being a connoisseur I naturally was more interested in the notice for Everard's Tiger beer, selling at a remarkable £1.30 per pint, though John quite correctly pointed out that it was only eleven o'clock and far too soon for lunchtime drinking. I was also impressed by the print of William Blake's *Tiger, Tiger* on one wall and the other framed scrolls, each of which commemorated some part of Wednesfield's history, such as the trap-making, the Battle of Wednesfield when the Anglo-Saxon forces reputedly fought off the Danish invaders, and the town in bygone days.

Probably the most famous person ever to come from Wednesfield is Tessa Sanderson, who won the gold medal in the javelin event at the Olympic Games of 1984 in Los Angeles. A new housing estate in Wednesfield is named Sanderson Park after her and its massive gate features her winning Olympic throw etched on it. Tessa is the daughter of a Jamaican couple who came to England in the middle of the century but have since returned to their homeland. She has been awarded the MBE in recognition of her achievements and holds honorary degrees from Birmingham and Wolverhampton Universities. In 1995 she even appeared in pantomime as the first ever black Fairy Godmother.

But she wasn't in Wednesfield on this particular day, at least not in The Royal Tiger, so, refreshed and warmed by our coffee, we decided it was time for us to move on. We rejoined the cut at the far end of the town and followed its course through pleasant housing estates. Many of the houses on this stretch have made a feature of the part of their land that backed on to the cut. There were some attractively landscaped gardens, with colourful shrubs, nodding daffodils and winter pansies, bench-seats and other signs that the residents of these houses valued their views on to the cut. This is certainly appreciated by the families of coots and moorhens that swim happily around here. You can tell from the expressions on their faces.

At midday we came off the towpath again to take a drink at the United Kingdom pub, where a relief manager pulled us half pints of Banks's and told us that he had recently given up his tenancy in Wednesfield because of the threat from The Royal Tiger. A curious coincidence.

An hour later we were out in countryside again but this was no tranquil stroll for the steady roar of traffic grew louder as we approached the M6. The Curly Wyrley actually runs parallel to the motorway for a few hundred yards and it was a curious experience to be walking alongside the growl of lorries and cars. Passing under the motorway on the towpath we came upon a permanent site for gipsies, where dogs on chains barked their warnings at us. The Black Country 'osses on the opposite side of the cut may well have been the property of this encampment but they looked just like all the other such 'osses we had seen on our travels.

At Sneyd Junction we turned south for the day's final stretch into Walsall. On the right the land is undeveloped and contains some small lakes but on the left heavy industry clanked noisily away, in tune with the motorway's noise. And a man was fishing serenely at one of these small lakes, as if he couldn't hear any of it.

Maybe he was deaf.

We were now heading for Walsall, so I started to tell John about the Leather Museum there and about the fact that Princess Anne's saddles were made personally for her by a firm in Walsall.

'I used to go out with her,' he chimed in, obviously intent on wresting the narrative away from me.

John is a fund of stories. He has an opinion on everything and at least one story to support each opinion.

'Well, at least everybody in Liverpool used to think so.'

'How come?' I asked innocently.

'We were performing a lot in London and we were presented to her at some do,' he explained. 'So, when we got back to Liverpool, I told everyone that I'd asked her out and she'd accepted. And they all believed me, even when she married Captain Foggo. I told them that she'd only got hitched to him as a cover-up because she couldn't admit to being with a commoner but that we still saw each other whenever we could.'

'And they believed you?' I said, genuinely surprised.

I had always been led to believe in the unfoolable sagacity of Scousers.

It is time I told you a bit more about my travelling companion, John Gorman. You know that he has been a successful entertainer in his time, initially as a member of the Liverpool pop group The Scaffold together with poet Roger McGough and Beatle Paul McCartney's brother who called himself Mike McGear. Later he was part of Grimms, another musical and entertainment act, and then he joined the resident team on the children's Saturday morning TV show *Tiswas* before working with many of the same team in another show entitled *O.T.T.*

He has enormous creative energy but it's his story-telling that I feel a need to illustrate for you here, because it was during this stretch of towpath from Sneyd Junction down towards Walsall that he regaled me with some of his more surreal tales.

'And I told them that the Queen Mum used to be our roadie.'

'You what?'

'Yeah. I said that she got bored in the Palace all day so, whenever we were in London, we used to give her a bell and she'd slip on an old coat and come and drive the van for us on a gig. And they used to ask why nobody recognised her and I'd tell them that she wore a disguise, like a false moustache and a flat cap. But she really used to enjoy driving round the south and living like a real person. She was specially fond of fish and chips, which, of course, she could never get at the Palace. Not proper fish and chips anyway.'

'And people believed you?' I queried. 'You don't mean this was part of your act?'

'No,' he said, looking so hurt at the implications of my question that I decided to quiz him no further.

Thus entertained, we passed by Birchills Junction where the Curly Wyrley heads off on its meandering route to the north east. There is a canal museum here but, naturally, being in league with the rest of the Black Country, it had closed at 12.30 p.m. and it was now 1.30 p.m. We joined the towpath on the Walsall Canal and walked past a series of eight locks and then past the old buildings of Smith's Flour Mill, sadly unused now but ripe for conversion into something like, maybe, an art gallery. We passed two sad-looking fishermen in the canal basin just beyond the mill and we headed down the Walsall Arm into the town itself.

It was difficult to contain our excitement.

SEVENTEEN

SADDLING UP IN WALSALL

What can you say about Walsall?

Whenever you hear the town's name mentioned on national radio or television, which, admittedly, isn't very often, it always sounds like they're talking about Warsaw, the capital of Poland. And, up until the recent collapse of communism in Eastern Europe, there were certain political similarities between Walsall and the eastern bloc. It's all history now but not so many years ago there was a faction of the Labour party in Walsall which was considered extremist by the national Labour party. There was the usual witch-hunt and banning of persons and all that kind of hoo-ha which politicians, particularly of the left, indulge in from time to time in order to prove that they are hard knocks. It happened in Russia under Stalin. It happened in Czechoslovakia after the Prague Spring of 1968. In fact, it happened all over Eastern Europe until Gorbachev's *perestroika* appeared out of the blue and led step by step to the collapse of the Berlin Wall, to the Velvet Revolution in Czechoslovakia, to the execution of Ceaucescu in Romania and so on and so forth.

But in the Black Country, at around about the time of these world-changing events, a group of Labour councillors decided that the next place for the Revolution was Walsall.

Unfortunately for them the tide of history and, more importantly, the tide of New Labour was turning. They were prohibited from holding office, meaning that there were two Labour parties operating in Walsall for a number of years.

The daft thing about all this is that one of the main platforms on which these so-called extremists stood was concerned with moving power away from the centre and creating local neighbourhood committees to decide local policy. And that is precisely what now happens, despite this proscription of the Labour councillors who first supported the notion.

So, for example, in Darlaston, which is one of the small towns that comes under the Walsall metropolitan umbrella, the Darlaston Central Local Committee, which sounds a bit like a Russian *soviet,* recently distributed a questionnaire through the library. It asked local residents for their views on the best and worst things about the town and about what improvements they would like to see.

Now, if I tell you that, as recently as the nineteen-eighties, Darlaston (or Darlo, as the locals wittily call it) was a major manufacturing town, when the closure of Rubery Owen, F.H. Lloyd, GKN and a number of other factories left thousands of workers suddenly redundant. If I tell you that in the eighteenth and nineteenth centuries it was the centre of the gun-making trade in England, and that at one time there were more than three hundred gunlock filers and more than fifty gunlock forgers active in the town, including Jonah Spittle and Cornelius

126

Whitehouse of Wednesbury (both of whom you'll meet later) and Thomas Rubery of Darlaston, whose descendants established Rubery Owen as a manufacturer of components for the cycle, motor vehicle and aviation industries. If I also tell you that the guns made in Darlaston were subsequently traded for slaves in Africa as part of the Golden Triangle of trading that brought untold wealth to the United Kingdom, which in turn brought the children of that slave trade back to Britain in the nineteen-fifties, -sixties and -seventies to face the hostility of the native citizens. If I tell you that Darlaston was renowned as a centre for bull-baiting, another of the unsavoury pastimes of our Black Country forebears, and that, until very recently, a Bull Stake was situated in the heart of the town to commemorate its inglorious past. If I tell you that one its most famous citizens was Rough Moey, who kept the Mine Borers' Arms in the town, who reputedly had a wooden leg, only one eye, and was a renowned barefist fighter and organiser of bull-baiting and cock-fighting contests in the town, and, to top things off, was the last man to sell his wife in Wednesbury Market.

If I tell you all this and show you the centre of modern day Darlaston, you will understand the need for local committees to make their voices heard. For modern day Darlaston is a total disgrace. Most of its shops are boarded up, awaiting purchase and refurbishment. Its nineteen-seventies shopping centre is, like so many others, little more than a wind tunnel. The most dominant building in Darlaston is its library, which stands proudly in the heart of the old town. It is not surprising that the citizens of Darlaston who bothered to fill in their questionnaires about their town voted the library as the best thing in town. More worryingly, the third most popular return was "Nothing's any good".

Anyway, that's just a little bit about Walsall politically. But, if you're not interested in that, what else is there about Walsall that's worth noting?

Well, there's the Leather Museum, which was nominated as Industrial Museum of the Year by National Heritage in 1990. Now, when you read that, it sounds impressive, until you realise that "nominated" doesn't mean "won". Still, fair play, it's there and we had to visit it.

'It's because of the royals,' John volunteered, as I shared my ignorance with him while steering him from The Wharf area across town to the museum.

'How d'you mean?' I asked, while waving my thanks to a lorry driver who had been forced to brake rather suddenly when we set off across what Walsall laughably calls a ring road.

'Didn't I read somewhere that the skins of the fattest cows in England are sent here to be made into saddles for the royals, especially for Annie?' he said, all wide-eyed.

'Where d'you read that?" I asked, curious as to the source of his information.

'*The Liverpool Echo*, of course,' he answered. 'It's gospel.'

John's recollection, surprisingly, turned out to be not far from the truth, though his insertion of the term "fattest" into his description of the cows' hides used to make saddlery for the Princess Royal was a bit anti-monarchist, to say the least.

Walsall's leather trade goes back centuries - well, two centuries. It used to be believed that the reason for this was that the leather industry grew out of the tanning industry but this is now disputed and it seems that the leather trade grew out of the town's history in lorinery.

This is not some quaint Marquis de Sade-style sexual deviation; it's ironmongery for horsemanship (though as far as I can see it's mostly women who ride horses nowadays) such as buckles, stirrups, bits, snaffles, studs, pendants, coach nails and so forth.

By the early part of the nineteenth century, it is clear that many of these loriners had widened their sphere of activity into leather trades, producing saddlery and harness goods in addition to the ironmongery with which they had been associated for many years. There are still over ninety companies in Walsall associated with the leather trade, one of which bears the wonderful name of Jabez Cliff, situated in what looks like a rundown Victorian factory alongside the aforementioned ring road that takes passing motorists very slowly through the town. It is the Jabez Cliff factory that is responsible for making the saddlery used by Princess Anne.

One of the by-products of Walsall's history in the leather trade is that its football team, at the time of our visit languishing at the bottom of Division One of the Football League, is universally known as "The Saddlers". The team has always been pretty average. To tell the truth, they have lived for sixty years on the memory of once beating Arsenal in the F.A.Cup in the nineteen-thirties. A few years ago they sold their then-stadium to property developers for a large sum of money and built a new stadium at Bescot, an area of Walsall that is quite close to the motorway. Last year, to celebrate the publication of a book about Walsall Football Club, a special bash was organised at Bescot Stadium, to which the great and the good of the Black Country were invited. Unfortunately, the invitation was typed on a word processor whose spellchecker substituted "Biscuit" for the unrecognised "Bescot". No one at the club noticed this error until after the invitations had been sent out.

Another thing about Walsall is its Arboretum, which is a sort of posh word for a park, though why Walsall should want to use posh words I do not know. Anyway, the Walsall Arboretum is the site of the annual autumnal Walsall Illuminations, when for six weeks it is transformed into a magical wonderland of electricity, with lakeside lights, state-of-the-art laser shows, floodlit gardens and over fifty animated light scenes of things like children's television and cartoon characters. This display takes over forty thousand light bulbs and fifty miles of cable to put together and it all adds up to a fantastic family night out. "Why not come," says the glossy, "and see the dazzling lights of Walsall Illuminations for yourself this year?"

It sets the pulse racing, doesn't it?

Well, for one Walsall family who saw the dazzling lights a couple of years back, it was probably the biggest surprise of their lives. Apparently, they had taken themselves off for a week's holiday in Blackpool in order to see the illuminations there and, because the weather wasn't all that great, decided to sign up for a Magical Mystery Tour one day. Can you imagine their surprise when it turned out that their Tour was to take them to the Walsall Illuminations?

There's a couple of other things that Walsall is famous for that I want to tell you about before we get to the most remarkable feature of the town.

First off, there's Noddy Holder. Remember Noddy? He was the lead singer with Slade, the nineteen-seventies glam rock band whose song titles tortured the English language in a way that hadn't been done since James Joyce. This led to outbursts from teachers claiming that Noddy and his boys were preventing children from learning to spell properly. Remember *Cum on Feel the Noyz*? And *Skweeze Me, Pleeze me*? And *Mama Weer All Crazee Now*? Yes, that's right. And Noddy was the one with the outrageous top hat with mirrors on it, the curly blond hair dangling round his shoulders, the Rupert Bear trousers and the Doc Martens. That's him. OK?

Now Noddy, otherwise known as Neville John Holder, was born and went to school in Walsall. His first band was the "N'Betweens" who later became "Ambrose Slade", then later still the legendary "Slade". They had tried a variety of guises before they became glam rock totems. They'd been a sixties' rock n' roll band and then a skinhead band before they adopted the flares, glittery tank tops and stack-heeled boots. Between nineteen seventy-one and nineteen seventy-four, Slade had a succession of major hit records but the one for which they will always be remembered at drunken office parties is the loud and raucous *Merry Xmas, Everybody*, which gets trotted out annually for our delight and irritation by every half-baked radio station and supermarket muzak machine. Apparently Noddy himself wrote it in about an hour, assisted by several pints of Banks's.

And it shows!

The point about Slade was that they were not serious. They have been described variously as "brickies in eyeliners" and "a proper geezers' band, dressed like the diddymen". That was their appeal. They dressed in the prevailing glam rock styles but their music was good old working class rock n' roll. After leaving Slade, Noddy became a disc jockey on Piccadilly Radio in Manchester and was recently cast as - would you believe it? - a music teacher in a television series called *The Grimleys*. This series is supposedly set in the Black Country, but Noddy is the only believable character in it as he speaks normally while surrounded by actors young and old straining their larynxes to imitate the Black Country accent and failing. The ghost of Beryl Reid's Marlene hovers ever present in their mouths.

A more recent Walsall export to the entertainment world is Meera Syal. She wrote and directed the modern film classic *Bhaji on the Beach* and is one of the brains behind that stunning comedy series *Goodness*

Gracious Me, where four Anglo-Asians, one of whom is Meera, take the micky uproariously out of Anglo-Asian attitudes. One of my favourite sketches is where the four Asian characters go out to a restaurant "for an English" and try to outdo each other in ordering the blandest dish they can think of. Meera has also written two novels, the first of which *Anita and Me* describes fictionally, disturbingly yet entertainingly her early days growing up in an Asian household in an all-white Walsall suburb.

Anyway, back to the Leather Museum, which we duly and dutifully visited. The first exhibit to greet you is the "Saddle of the Month", which this month was a particular police saddle, all on its own in its special glass cabinet. We were then given a non-stop tour of Walsall's leather history by Ron, who had worked in the trade for fifty years and was now in his tenth year as a volunteer guide. Ron's enthusiasm was contagious and I didn't think I'd be able to tear John away as they discussed the finer points of currying and combing.

We were surprised to see handbags, purses, wallets, briefcases, suitcases and other goods on display, having expected to find only saddles and other horsy leatherwork. This was explained to us by another of the volunteer demonstrators in the upstairs part of the building, which had once been a leatherworking factory. Maureen was busy doing something to a small piece of leather and told us that she had spent all her working life making light leather goods in a factory called D. Mason's, that was now closed. She used to work from eight in the morning till six at night, making handbags, purses and belts. If there was a rush on, she could expect to work till seven thirty at night. If there was a really big rush, she could be tempted by the promise of a bacon sandwich to give up her Saturday morning and occasionally her Sunday afternoon.

Those were the days, eh? Poor but happy. Exploited by the D. Masons of the world who, you can be very sure, didn't work those hours themselves.

The highlight of the exhibition I have left till the end. You won't be surprised to learn that it was none other than the leather football with which the Walsall football team beat the famous Arsenal 2-0 in 1933. A Walsall friend of mine tells me that this, for Walsall folk, was more important than Hitler's invasion of Poland!

We left the Leather Museum infused with new knowledge and glad to have met Ron and Maureen, who was a charmer, particularly when she told us how she had learned to exaggerate her Black Country accent when there were visitors because they expected her to conform to their expectations. She also told us that, every time she saw Princess Anne on the television with the leather strap of her leather handbag tied in a knot at her shoulder, she wanted to slap her face for not having it properly reduced in size!

Anyway, we headed back to the centre of the town and back towards The Wharf area, where the best thing about Walsall is to be found. And I don't mean the new bus station which had yet to be opened but which apparently cost almost as much as the New Art Gallery to build. It looks like someone's idea of a spaceship from the nineteen-fifties and it's ghastly. When you look at it, you're reminded of all those crappy B-features at the cinema you used to see as a kid, when these spaceships landed on some planet and aliens with six legs and spider-heads came out from secret tunnels to attack them. Isn't it funny the way that aliens always spoke English in those films? And another thing – why are aliens always portrayed as being ugly and unpleasant? They could be perfectly nice, for all we know. They might have six legs and spider-heads but that's no reason to think they don't have things in common with the rest of us. They might be really cuddly and wear orange trainers on all their feet and silver lurex jackets, just like humans who shop from the catalogue.

Before we got to The Wharf, we had to pause on what is known as The Bridge in the middle of the shopping centre to look at the statuary there. In some ways, the statues that haunt the centres of our towns and cities define them too. Think of the Earl of Dudley and Duncan Edwards in the centre of Dudley and of Billy Wright and Prince Albert in Wolverhampton.

Anyway, first of all in Walsall there is a statue depicting Sister Dora, a nurse who in Victorian times did good works for the people of Walsall, like tending to the many victims of smallpox in the isolation hospital and nursing people who were disfigured in industrial accidents. Sister Dora, whose real name was Dorothy Pattinson, was a friend of the Warwickshire novelist, George Eliot, and some people have claimed that the character Dorothea in Eliot's *Middlemarch* is based on Walsall's own Angel of Mercy. It is said that, when Sister Dora died, the whole town went into mourning and several years later they decided to erect a statue in her memory.

Sadly, Sister Dora's statue is always covered in pigeon shit and every time you see it one of the pigeons responsible is perched right on top of her head, emptying its bowels, which does rather beg the question - "What is the point of pigeons?" I don't mean the sort that can be trained to fly prodigious distances with a metal ring attached to one leg, but the common-or-garden, fat, local variety that hang about in towns, making a nuisance of themselves – a bit like adolescent youths really. A town council elsewhere in England has recently proposed hiring sparrowhawks to eliminate its pigeon population and I'm pretty sure that poor old Sister Dora would heartily approve of a solution like that.

Anyway, why don't they put up statues of Noddy Holder and Meera Syal in Walsall? After all, they've both been awarded the MBE.

(That's a laugh, isn't it? Members of the Order of the British Empire. What Empire? I bet Meera enjoys the irony of it all) in recent years, so they've been more recognised by the nation than by their own town.

At the opposite side to this open patch between shopping precincts, which is called The Bridge because at one time that is exactly what it was – a bridge over running water, there is The Hippo. This is a stone hippopotamus approximately three feet high, set into the paving stones. No one knows why it's there or what it represents but, at night, it is the meeting place for the skateboard-anoraks.

Yes, that's right, those oddly-dressed youths with grossly baggy trousers and grossly baggy shirts who come out to play in town centres in the twilight hours after the shoppers have gone home and before the local drunks take over the streets. Like all societies, the skateboarders are an exclusive group. Membership is by invitation only and a special language has to be learned before you can even be considered. Here are a few of their terms, just in case you're ever tempted to apply for membership: grinding, sliding, frollocks, flips, shuve-its, and things to ollie. Really cool skateboarders are always on the look-out for wicked steps, gaps and banks, half pipes, sloped blocks, half curbs and mini ramps. Deserted shopping malls, supermarket car parks, and school playgrounds are favourite sites for cool skateboarders. Oh, and they have to have a meeting place.

In Walsall, it's The Hippo.

Unfortunately for us, when we got to The Bridge, neither Sister Dora nor The Hippo were there. Apparently they had been removed and taken away for a spring clean. Someone must have known we were coming!

One penultimate thing I ought to mention about Walsall, or at least one that Walsall wants to have mentioned about itself as part of its attempt to find an identity, is that it is the birthplace of the writer Jerome K. Jerome, of *Three Men in a Boat* fame. I have never read this book, nor do I know anyone else who has. Furthermore, I have no particular desire to read this book, nor, I suspect, does anyone in Walsall nowadays. And, let's face it, Jerome K. Jerome had no particular desire to remember Walsall. The family moved away when he was two years old and he only came back to visit the town twice in his lifetime, once because he was invited back to receive a scroll giving him the Freedom of the Borough of Walsall. So, despite the fact that there is a small museum near the town centre devoted to the said Jerome K. Jerome, we headed in the opposite direction.

EIGHTEEN

ROGUE'S GALLERY

And this was to the *piéce de resistance* of our short stay in Walsall - the recently-opened New Art Gallery Walsall, standing proudly and luminously at the end of The Wharf.

It's a bit of a freak, to be honest, this Art Gallery. It opened in February 2000, built with nearly sixteen million quid of lottery money and design by architects with an apparently international renown. It houses three hundred and fifty works of art by one hundred and fifty three artists, including Braque, Cezanne, Constable, Degas, Gaugin, Van Gogh, Matisse, Millet, Modigliani, Picasso, Renoir, Rodin, Turner and Whistler. And those are just some of the more famous names.

So where did all this lot come from? And why did it all end up in Walsall of all places?

Well, it is known as the Garman Ryan collection, because it consists of works collected by Kathleen Garman and Sally Ryan. And who are they? Well, Kathleen Garman was the mistress of the sculptor Jacob Epstein for thirty-four years, during which time she bore him three children, until he eventually married her in 1955, and Sally Ryan was an American sculptor and faithful disciple of Epstein's.

So what's it got to do with Walsall?

Allow me to spell it out. Kathleen Garman came from nearby Wednesbury, where her father was Medical Officer of Health. A talented musician, she went to London at the age of twenty and there met Epstein who was forty-one, married, and at the height of his controversial career. Epstein was the child of Polish Jews, who had settled in New York in the middle of the nineteenth century. After the usual precocious childhood (the sort that we never had), he pursued an artistic career in Paris and then settled in London, where he was commissioned to produce a series of sculptures for the British Medical Association building on the Strand. One of these eighteen sculptures, entitled *Maternity* and featuring a semi-naked pregnant woman, received massive hostile publicity. The *Evening Standard* declared it to be something that "no careful father would wish his daughter, or no discriminating young man his fiancé, to see." Honestly, you'd think they were talking about *Lady Chatterley's Lover*! When a few years later, Epstein's sculpture for the tomb of Oscar Wilde featured prominent genitalia, as art-anoraks are wont to call them, his reputation as a scandal-raiser was confirmed.

Kathleen Garman, as is evident from early photographs of her and from Epstein's bronze bust executed in 1921, was a strikingly beautiful young woman when they first met. Maybe the Warsaw/Walsall consonance was what brought them together. Or maybe it was the link between her father's occupation as Medical Officer of Health and the sculptor's work for the British Medical Association building. Whatever, she was a looker and he was a randy old goat. He had already fathered a child by the actress Meum Lindsell-Stewart, whom his first wife Margaret had brought up as her own. And there had been a succession of other female "house guests" living with the Epsteins for extended periods of time. And he later, in 1934, had a child by another woman. Kathleen bore him Theodore in 1924, Kitty in 1926 and Esther in 1929 and remained devoted to him all her life, although she didn't live with him until his first wife Margaret died in 1947 and even then it took eight years to get him to finally marry her.

No doubt Epstein would have considered himself to be an artist beyond the constraints of normal society, though quite where this unwritten law of the artistic community came from I do not know. Mind you, Kathleen wasn't the only Garman girl to have a bit of a racy love life. Her sister Lorna married the wealthy publisher Lawrence Wishart when she was sixteen, then, while holidaying in Cornwall with her children, saw the young Laurie Lee playing his fiddle and called out "Boy, come and play for me". His playing began a long-term affair, during which she inspired many of his best-known poems and, when he went to join the armed struggle in Spain, she used to send him pound notes dabbed with Chanel No.5. She bore Lee a daughter, Yasmin, who was brought up with her other children by Wishart. Not content with this bit of slap and tickle, Lorna later chucked Laurie Lee in favour of a twenty-one year old painter Lucien Freud, who painted her as *Girl with a Daffodil.*

Now Epstein may have been a rogue when he was alive, but when he died in 1959 he did leave Kathleen a huge collection of works of art. Under the terms of his will, his collection of tribal and classical sculpture was sold off, presumably to provide funds to support Kathleen. But there was a number of other works that she retained and later added to.

At some stage, and no one quite knows when or why, she began to collaborate with Sally Ryan on what was to become the Garman Ryan collection. She had wanted the collection to be displayed in the old family home in Wednesbury but unfortunately that building had been demolished and so she offered the works to Walsall. For many years they were in an upstairs room of Walsall Public Library but this was always an inadequate space for their display. This, then, is the reason for the magnificent New Art Gallery Walsall situated at the end of the same canal basin where we had arrived some time earlier but which we were now finally to enter and explore.

Now, I have to say that neither of us was overimpressed with the exterior of the building and its terracotta tiling, as we approached it from the towpath. Nor were we that impressed with the Gallery Square, which, according to the Art Gallery literature, is "bold, unapologetic and plain speaking" but which, according to John, is actually just a space for litter to blow around in.

But inside it is a different story. At ground floor level there is the wonderful Discovery Gallery designed to draw children into art work by offering them some fascinating artistic activities such as puppetry, spin painting à la Damien Hirst, or observational drawing of leather shoes made in Walsall (nice touch, that). The first and second floors house the Garman Ryan collection, displayed thematically in a series of interconnecting rooms each with its own vari-sized window. The range of work is stunning, the effects of the light from these windows on the art are equally staggering, and the whole display makes you want to go home and tear down all those cheap prints you've used to decorate your own house.

If I had the choice, there are three works that I would probably kill for to have on my walls at home. These are Modigliani's magnificently moody *Caryatid*, which leaps out of its frame and illuminates the room in which it is placed; Buffet's *Small Girl Reading a Book* – those eyes peering over the top of the pages are just so full of childlike wonder; and Braque's *Birds in Flight*, because it just reminds me of all that birdy freedom I so envy.

I could go on about the temporary Blue exhibition on the third floor with its Picasso, its Chagall, its Derek Jarman audio-visual and all its other wonders but I won't, because by the time this book appears it will have been replaced by another exhibition. I could tell you about the spectacular views of Walsall and the rest of the Black Country from its fourth floor restaurant, which surely must serve the most interesting food in Walsall, but I won't, because I want to keep it as a secret for myself.

What I will say is that you should go there. And go there again and again, as I intend to do. It is magnificent and it is free. And all you wannabe-millionaires who buy lottery tickets have paid for it.

And the announcements in the lift are recordings of Noddy Holder's voice.

NINETEEN

LOCKED OUT OF WILLENHALL

The Abbey Manor Guest House in Walsall where we stayed that night is next door to the Acacia Hotel, although when you go through the front door it is quite clearly one property. Two front doors, two names, but only one reception desk. We puzzled on this all evening.

Next morning Pauline, our landlady, put us out of our misery.

'Next door used to be a doctors' surgery but the doctors moved and the man who owns the Abbey Manor bought it and had it converted. Then unfortunately he had a heart attack and the lady who used to manage the Abbey Manor resigned because she couldn't cope with the two properties. And that's why Mike, my husband, and I are here now,' she said.

As I have pointed out before, there is always an explanation for everything in the Black Country. It may not be totally satisfactory – for instance, I still was no clearer about why one property should have two names and two entries in Walsall's Guest Houses and Hotels Guide but only one door, only one phone number and only one set of prices. But it was an explanation, gleaned over the breakfast table, and it was all I was going to get.

For the first time on our travels we encountered other guests at the Abbey Manor (or was it the Acacia?). And our rooms each had en suite facilities *and* a duvet *and* a telephone with an external line. Clearly, we had landed in the lap of luxuriousness.

The previous evening we had walked into the town looking for somewhere to eat and had passed two Indian restaurants offering special menus on Wednesday and Thursday (and, of course, we were here on Tuesday) before settling on one called the Royal India. The meal we had had was okay but it didn't compare with the previous evening's superb repast at the Bilash Tandoori in Wolverhampton. We had asked for Cobra beer and, when told there was none in stock, settled for Carlsberg but mysteriously, by the time I needed a refill, Cobra beer had sneaked (or should that be snaked?) into the Royal India.

So that morning's fried breakfast was particularly welcome and fortified us for the next stages of our journey. The fourth day was due to be the longest walk because I was keen to take in a couple of small Black Country towns on the way and that meant leaving the towpath for extended periods.

Experienced trekkers by now, we quickly packed and soon rejoined the cut. On our way again. Walsall was quite quickly left behind as we headed towards where the cut passes under the M6 motorway again. Very heavy industrial plants lined the one side of the cut on the approach to the motorway but, from the canalside, it is impossible to tell what is being manufactured there.

'In America there'd be signs saying "Welcome to Washer Country",' John said. 'Or "You are now passing the world's biggest nuts and bolts factory".'

I could see what he meant. We are terribly unproud about what we do to earn our livings in the Black Country.

'I've felt that all the way,' I replied. 'It's the lack of signposting. Remember those interpretation boards about the glass industry in Stourbridge? They ought to have those all along the side of the cut.'

It's a thought, you know. I suppose someone will say that they'd get vandalised and that no one ever passes through either by water or by towpath so it would be a waste of time. Well, how do they know if they haven't tried it? And what are they doing to encourage more traffic?

But I was getting carried away in my imagination now, holding heated debates with fictional councillors who all looked like that ancient actor that played Councillor Duxbury in the film of *Billy Liar*. We strode over the aqueduct that carries the cut over the trickle of water known as the River Tame, which used to be a major thoroughfare before the canal age. I was so busy with my thoughts that I almost missed the eerie Darlaston cemetery which looked strangely out of place in the industrial hinterland beyond the M6.

Our first port of call was to be Willenhall, one-time lock-making capital of England. This meant we had to leave the towpath at the Midland Road Bridge (no, there wasn't a lock!) and pass an example of what is happening to much of the Black Country. On the site of former factories huge new warehouses are being built, one of which proudly proclaims that it is to be a sortation centre. Now, I can't find this word in any dictionary of mine. I assume it means 'distribution' because that quite clearly is what it's for. It's a place where goods will be stockpiled prior to being transported elsewhere in the kingdom. Nothing will be made there. No one will get very dirty. It's an illustration of how the Black

Country is changing from a manufacturing economy to a service one.

As we walked on, I mused gently to myself about this neologism, sortation. If industrialists can make up their own words without a by-your-leave, then why can't anyone? Of course, that's exactly what happens, particularly in the world of advertising. And we're not in France, where the Academie Francaise attempts but fails to prevent terms such as *le weekend* coming out of the mouths of French children. So I invented my own term – fartation, a place where politicians go to exchange their bags of wind.

Well, why not?

It was a steady half mile walk into the centre of Willenhall, which we entered via a bridge across railway lines and past a huge building called West Midland House. This is now the home of over a hundred small businesses but it was once the factory premises of Josiah Parkes & Sons, lockmakers. And it was Willenhall's tradition for lock-making that had made me insist we visit.

The town began as a lock-making centre during the reign of Queen Elizabeth I, when it was granted the monopoly of making all the locks required by the state. No, nothing to do with chastity belts, before you snigger! Locks were made by mastersmiths in small workshops at the back of their homes. The industry was a family one, with many locksmiths employing apprentices from nearby workshops. Willenhall used to be known as "Humpshire" because of the deformities in many of the lock-makers caused by the position they worked in. Allegedly many of the pubs in the town had seats which were specially designed for these oddly-shaped locksmiths. There are still nineteen Lock Manufacturers listed in the Yellow Pages directory and Willenhall retains ninety per cent of the employment of the lock industry in the United Kingdom. But that industry is shrinking fast as mass manufacturing of locks can now be done more cheaply and cost-effectively elsewhere in the world. Although there are still some rather oddly-shaped people in Willenhall!

I knew there was a Lock Museum in Willenhall, which is situated in a former locksmith's Victorian house and workshop, but when we got there we found it was, of course, locked! The private museum houses, we are told, an "interesting collection of locks and keys" – surprise, surprise! We had come on one of the few days it was open but opening time was eleven o'clock and it was only just after ten. So we headed back to the centre of the town towards the library which also supposedly had a display about the lock-making history of the town. Sadly for us it too was locked, Wednesday being the day when the good burghers of Willenhall are forbidden to read books.

We tried the doors of the new J.D. Wetherspoon pub called The Malthouse, situated in a building that had until recently been a bingo hall and before that a cinema. I guessed that, if it was anything like its Wednesfield counterpart, it would house framed accounts of Willenhall's history. Sadly, it too was locked until eleven o'clock. You do have to say that Willenhall's tradition with locks is being very well maintained!

What else was there for us to do? Fortunately, Willenhall has an attractive town centre, most of which is pedestrianised and preserved as a conservation area, where a market is held every Wednesday, Friday and Saturday. And today was Wednesday – we were in luck!

We strolled through the busy streets, past the old clock tower and through the stalls that sold everything you could ever imagine wanting and plenty that you could never imagine wanting. Outside a butcher's shop, a young man in bloodied apron was offering "Four breasts for two forty nine and get your legs free", while from a market stall nearby a trader was trying to entice us with large trifles.

Tempting, eh?

The market seemed to stretch on for ever, winding through the narrow streets. It was full of shoppers and was what I imagine markets used to be like in ye olden days.

Now, I am here going to award the prize for best hairdressers' name to Willenhall. Hairdressers seem to have this penchant for trying to outdo each other in the naffness of the names they choose for their salons (or shops, as they're called in the Black Country). So we've got Ali Barbers, Goldie-Locks and Rapunzel in Wolverhampton. There's Beyond the Fringe in Walsall. There's City Snippers and Crowning Glory in West Bromwich. There's Clipjoint Hair Design and Cut N Dried in Wednesfield. There's Hair & Now by Julie in Oldbury and Hair Doos in Dudley. There's Hairline in Rowley Regis, Hairport in Kingswinford, Hair Today in Brierley Hill, and Hairwaves in Oldbury. Then there's Headmasters in Netherton, Mane Street in Gornal and the Tipton duo of It's a Snip and Kroppers.

I was very tempted by Herr Flick in Bilston and even more by Curl Up 'N' Dye in Brierley Hill but in the end Willenhall wins it for its outstanding trio of Deb 'n' Hair, Hair Raisers and Scissorhands. You just know that, in salons with names like that, your hair is safe.

Unless, of course, Shazzer, Mazzer and Shagger are now snipping there!

We stopped off at The Bell pub for a cup of coffee. There the landlady and a friend from the market were plotting a girls' night out because their blokes were going out on a breakfast trip which included a stripper. What is it with these breakfast trips in the Black Country? Is it that they need their cholestorol in order to handle the rest of the entertainment – Uttoxeter races for the Tipton gang and a stripper for this Willenhall bunch? Or is it that their health-conscious wives and girlfriends won't let them have fry-ups at home? Or is there something more sinister going on that has entirely escaped my attention?

I think we should be told.

Back on the towpath, for quite a stretch now we were walking in parallel with the new Black Country Route, which was built in the early nineteen nineties and cuts a swathe through the industrial West Midlands from the A4123 Birmingham New Road to Junction 10 on the M6 motorway. The most interesting feature of this road, apart from the fact that, if you're in a hurry and it's not Friday afternoon, it speeds you across the Black Country at a great rate of knots, are the sculptures which flash by from time to time. At first, you're not quite sure what they are but then you get curious and you want to investigate. You can't see all of these eighteen sculptures from the side of the cut so it was just as well that I'd got a leaflet about them from Bilston Museum the day before. The first one visible is the towering 'House of Birds', which is a series of interconnected bird boxes astride a huge trunk, designed apparently to celebrate the birds that used to nest in the area.

At my instigation, we came off the towpath at the Barnes Meadow Bridge and cut back along the side of the Black Country New Road to its junction with the Black Country Route, known as the Lunt Junction. In the middle of the road island here there is a large mound topped by a huge wooden sculpture looking like the launch pad for some invisible space rocket.

'It's called 'Bilston Oak',' I read. 'It's meant to represent the old forest of Bilston re-emerging from the stump of a massive oak tree.'

Oak trees have been planted in the centre of the sculpture to represent a new beginning and the early shoots of these are now beginning to waft above the structure.

'Oh, yes,' said John. 'Pretty good, but not half as impressive as the black horse over there.'

He pointed to the opposite side of the road where the black figure of a mounted horse sprang from the tufted grass and glowed dully in the morning haze.

'That's called 'Horse and Rider',' I read again - I was getting quite good at this. 'It's meant to represent the spirit of Bilston making its way through the centuries to the 'Bilston Oak', which represents the future.'

'I like it,' said John. 'That's the first thing you've shown me that isn't harking back to the past. Come on. It's time to move on.'

He can be so prosaic at times. But I followed him back to the cut where we resumed our walk, which now took us parallel with the Black Country New Road, that other major transportation route designed to bring about the regeneration of the Black Country.

This road has an interesting background. It was the creation of an unelected government agency, the Black Country Development Corporation, which was set up in 1987 by the Conservative government to transform the area and to pave the way for a second Industrial Revolution. Its mission was to create jobs, to build new houses and new roads, and to set in train a new working and living environment. It was given considerable powers to bypass local authorities in matters of the compulsory purchase of land and the granting of planning applications and was at first treated with great suspicion by the largely-Labour councils of the area. Mind you, those same Labour councils made sure they got their people on to its Board of Directors. The Black Country Development Corporation adopted an aggressive marketing style in order to win people over to what they were doing, with slogans like "Black Country bites back" and "The Industrious Revolution".

Subtle stuff, eh!

The Black Country New Road is at the centre of this development. It is surrounded already by new business parks, which have spread like a rash along its length, and it throbs continuously with the sound of heavy traffic.

We followed its path for some distance, admiring the new housing estates that have grown up along the canalside and wondering how attractive an environment this was to live in, given the constant roar of traffic. As attractive perhaps as those old cottages, now no longer standing, that would have once occupied similar sites.

This stretch was made more memorable for us by the mark of SOCIAL VOMIT, a distinctive piece of graffiti that is sprayed on to every canal bridge between Willenhall and Wednesbury. And, when you look at some of the dereliction and waste that still exists around these parts, you have to say that its anonymous author has a point.

SOCIAL VOMIT's last appearance just happened to be at our next scheduled stop, near a town at the heart of the Black Country and where the cut first appeared – Wednesbury.

TWENTY

BEING REASONABLE IN WEDNESBURY

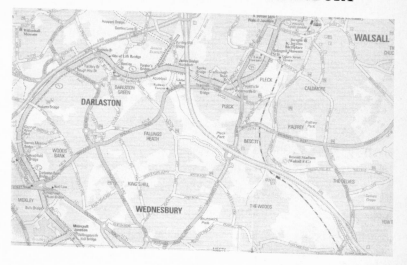

Wednesbury is a place which is well known to all motorists and lawyers. First of all, it's the name motorists see on the road sign just before they get to Junction 9 on the M6 motorway and they're stuck once again in a queue of traffic and they can see that sign which says THAT'LL BE THE DAEWOO and they're cursing Buddy Holly for ever having recorded that blasted song *That'll be the Day* and they're looking at their watches and they're wondering why they ever came on this road when they knew it would be like that.

Secondly, as any half-decent law student knows, Wednesbury is famous in legal circles for the term "Wednesbury reasonableness", which apparently is a classic reference regarding what is reasonable and fair: this stemmed from a legal case involving the intended opening hours of a cinema in Wednesbury.

Daft really. The cinema had become a bingo hall before the case was resolved!

Not really. I just made that up.

Wednesbury is, of course, named after the Saxon god Woden, who was particularly powerful and effective in the middle of the week, hence Wednesday. When William the Conqueror commissioned his Domesday Book to ascertain the extent of his kingdom, Wednesbury was probably the most populated place in the Midlands. According to Domesday, there were an estimated ninety-six people living there in the eleventh century, compared with thirty-two in Birmingham and forty-six in West Bromwich (and those forty-six form the hard core of West Bromwich Albion F.C.'s support to this very day!). But that wasn't the main reason I felt we had to visit Wednesbury or Wedgebury, as the local history books claim it's pronounced, though I've never come across anybody who calls it that.

We had to visit Wednesbury, because that was where the first stretch of Brindley's original cut went from Birmingham. And if it was good enough for Brindley, it was good enough for us. It was also at Wednesbury that the famous Thirty Foot Coal Seam was particularly close to the surface, so that colliers could dig huge amounts of it from the ground easily, though we had no plans to go coal mining! And it was to get speedy access to this coal that Matthew Boulton and the "Lunaticks", who sponsored this first stretch of cut, wanted. However, this stretch, known as the Wednesbury Oak Loop after Telford's cut changed the course of the main route by cutting through the Coseley Tunnel, has long been closed.

Our target was the most prominent geographical point in Wednesbury - St. Bartholomew's church, which became visible as soon as we climbed up from the towpath at Willingsworth Hall Bridge. It is built on the hill where archaeology-anoraks say there once stood an Anglo-Saxon fort, the stronghold of King Alfred's daughter, Aethelfleda. So we headed through the brand new industrial units of the Automotive Products Park, built on land previously occupied by the giant Patent Shaft works - another casualty of the early 1980s - and across the equally new Black Country New Road and up the hill to the parish church of St. Bartholomew's.

Wednesbury used to be known as "Tube Town", not because of the number of TVs in use there but because it was where wrought iron and later steel tubes were manufactured extensively in a number of local factories, the biggest of which was Patent Shaft. This was down to an invention in Wednesbury by one Cornelius Whitehouse (remember him?), whose father had been a renowned weapons maker at Wednesbury Forge and who himself was on the list of gun-makers at neighbouring Darlaston. Our Cornelius invented a method of making wrought iron tubes which was cheaper than that used previously and which produced tubes that were twice as long. There was a huge demand in the early nineteenth century for pipes to carry coal gas, which was just beginning to be used to light factories. A further development of this was the invention of an improved shaft as an axle, initially for horse-drawn vehicles and later for the railway industry.

Most of this industry, like Patent Shaft, has gone down the tube now. The biggest employers in Wednesbury are the Swedish furniture store IKEA and the do-it-yourself store B & Q. And a parcel firm is just opening a new Call Centre there, which will also employ a lot of people. And you know what I think about Call Centres!

The church's blackened exterior shows better than any written description what the fires of industry poured out into the atmosphere. And now, to add new insult to old injury, its walls are daubed with graffiti, its stained glass windows covered with anti-vandal plastic sheeting, its churchyard overgrown, the grass between its ancient gravestones barely kept under control, and its drains and water-channels are home to empty two-litre cider bottles and Strongbow cans. It has become the hang-out for a godless generation of youths who vent their anger towards society on this symbol of the past.

Now, I'm no churchgoer but I felt sad in the grounds of this church. I was glad, therefore, that inside St. Bartholomew's is everything that outside is not. Dating originally from medieval times but developed mostly in the nineteenth century, the church is a wonder. It has fifteen stunning stained glass windows, their blues and yellows and reds glowing despite their external vandal-proofing and it has the most famous lectern in the Black Country in the shape, not of the traditional eagle, but of a fighting cock complete with spurs and shaven comb.

'You won't have heard this song, will you?' I said to John, who was stroking the lectern in awe and wonder.

'What's that?' he asked.

I launched into my vaguely-remembered rendition of the opening of the eighteenth-century ballad, *The Wedgebury Cocking*:

"At Wednesbury there was a cocking,
  A match between Newton and Scroggins;
The colliers and nailers all left work,
  And all to Spittle's went jogging.
  To see this noble sport,
  Many noblemen resorted;
And though they'd but little money,
  Yet that little they freely sported."

'Yes, very good,' he said. 'So now I suppose you're going to bore me with the history of cockfighting in Wednesbury.'

'Funny you should mention that,' I said.

Cockfighting was probably introduced by the Romans and by the eighteenth century it had become a major sport in England, and particularly so in the Black Country. Cocks were specially fed and trained for fighting. When they were one year old, they were "dubbed", that is, their combs and wattles were removed. They were mature at two to three years of age, weighing between three and a half and four and a half pounds. Ten days before a fight there was further intensive feeding and training to get the birds into the best possible shape for fighting. In the fight, two birds were placed in a pit, which was usually a circular area surrounded by a low wooden wall, bets would be placed, then the cocks were released to fly at each other, striking downwards with their metal spurs until one or the other was mortally wounded.

Along with barefist boxing and bull baiting, cockfighting was another cruel sport of a time when less value was placed on life. Cockfighting was banned in 1848 but the last Black Country prosecution was as recent as 1969 when twenty men were brought to trial for holding a quail fight in the backyard of a Wolverhampton house.

Wednesbury can also lay claim to being a key site in the development of Methodism in the Black Country. John and Charles Wesley, the founders of Methodism, both preached in Wednesbury between 1742 and 1743 and found many supporters willing to listen to what they had to say. Their message about living a good life being more important than the trappings of wealth so often associated with the established church found ready listeners in the rapidly-changing industrial community the Wesleys found in Wednesbury and the surrounding area. Of course, their popularity soon upset the clerics in the High Church and the local gentry who saw their own status threatened and who turned their parishioners against the messages being preached.

In October 1743 John Wesley came again to Wednesbury to preach but the house where he was staying was surrounded by an angry mob. He was forcibly taken to the home of a local magistrate who refused to do anything to appease them.

'What have I to do with Mr. Wesley?' he is reported as saying, as he dismissed the heckling crowd from his gates.

Wesley was then taken to the home of another magistrate where the crowd hoped to get better justice, but again they were denied. Back on the road again, they met up with another mob from Walsall and a huge fight began – rather like the sort of thing that happens nowadays when Wolves and Albion supporters meet. However, Wesley kept preaching and praying throughout all this riot and his calmness so impressed one of his opponents, a certain barefist boxer and local ruffian called George Clifton, that he swapped sides and carried Wesley on his back to safety. This man, hereafter known as Honest Munchin, was received into the Methodist society where he became a different man.

Whatever you think about Methodism or about organised religion in any of its manifestations, you have to say that John Wesley was a remarkable man and it is no surprise that Methodism became well established in the Black Country, along with other Non-Conformist groupings, despite or maybe because of this inauspicious beginning.

'Okay, so now what?' John wanted to know. 'Back to the cut?' He was getting the words right now.

'Not yet. A pint in the Old Blue Ball first,' I answ[...]
old pub. From the song. It can't be far, because th[...]
Bartholomew's used to slip out to the Blue Ball during ve[...]
to place a bet on a favourite cock while Jonah Spittle wa[...]

'Okay, let's go and see,' said John.

So, we went to the Old Blue Ball, which from the outside is a rather nondescript building despite its history. The landlord told us that, as well as being at the centre of the cockfighting game, it had once acted as a courthouse where a travelling judge would sit and settle disputes.

'A bloke was 'ung over there,' he told us. 'There's a chap comes in 'ere knows all abaht it. Writ a book. 'Istory book.'

Just then, however, his eye was taken by the arrival of three of his regular customers, who demanded his attention.

We took our pints of Bateman's beer and our cheese-and-onion sandwiches to a table by the window, where we enjoyed our repast and listened to the deeply-analytical discussion at the bar which centred on the performance of West Bromwich Albion in the previous evening's football match against Ipswich Town.

'They wus crap,' said the oldest of the three.

'Ar, they wus,' replied one of the others, pouring beer into his mouth.

'Ar,' agreed the third.

This passes for a lengthy dialogue in Wednesbury. Who said the art of conversation was dead? Perhaps it was just as well that the history-man never showed.

There's another even older pub in Wednesbury called Ye Olde Leathern Bottle, said to have been built in the early sixteenth century and visited by the highwayman Dick Turpin, but who knows whether there is any truth to that story? Maybe the history-man had gone there

. his lunchtime tipple.

Oh, there are two other things you might find interesting about Wednesbury. Janice with the giant beehive hair-do came from here, who used to say in her wonderful accent "Oi'll give it foive" on that long-ago television programme *Thank Your Lucky Stars* when new pop records were showcased. And its M.P. once was the vanishing John Stonehouse. Yes, that John Stonehouse, who was Postmaster General in Harold Wilson's Labour government and who disappeared in December 1974, leaving his clothes and shoes on the beach at Miami. He was discovered some five weeks later by Australian police who thought he was Lord Lucan and brought back home to face the music (probably *The Wedgebury Cocking*!). It turned out that he had obtained two passports in the names of the husbands of two widows in Wednesbury and planned to start a new life with his House of Commons secretary, the raven-haired Sheila Buckley. The Dictionary of National Biography calls him a "politician and confidence trickster".

It is not recorded what Wednesbury people called him.

Wednesbury is now represented in parliament by Betty Boothroyd, the ex-Windmill dancer who became the first female Speaker of the House of Commons in 1992 and whose matronly calls for order have brought her worldwide fame since the televising of the proceedings of the House commenced.

Shortly after our walk, Betty announced her retirement from the post of Speaker so it seems unlikely that she will choose to stage a disappearing act like her predecessor but who knows? Our Betty might yet trip the Light Fantastic again and high-step her way out of political life (and Wednesbury), maybe resurfacing as a belly-dancer in some Moroccan bazaar.

At least she won't get mistaken for Lord Lucan!

TWENTY ONE

THROUGH BANDIT COUNTRY TO SOHO

After saying goodbye to SOCIAL VOMIT in Wednesbury, we headed under the railway to Ocker Hill, where the Tame Valley Canal begins its long loop northwards to Brownhills and its junction with the Curly Wyrley.

The cut follows closely the line of the Black Country New Road from Ocker Hill all the way to Great Bridge where civilization as we know it ended until a huge new Asda store opened in 1988. This certainly increased job opportunities in the area but Great Bridge centre itself is still trying to figure out how to be part of this new dispensation.

For, just beyond Great Bridge Bridge (which my computer refuses to accept as real) we entered Bandit Country. A series of eight locks takes the cut up to Ryders Green Junction and at the bottom of these locks we met our first narrowboat traffic jam. A tall, wiry-looking bloke was standing on the towpath holding the shell of a narrowboat into the side bank with a rope while a dumpy woman was standing at the controls of a second boat. Ahead of them a middle-aged couple were taking their boat into this first lock.

We hadn't had any human contact for a while, so, keen to engage in some social chit-chat, we approached these people. But our hopes for whimsical conversations about messing about in boats were put paid to immediately.

'It's Bandit Country rahnd 'ere,' the tall bloke began glumly. 'Yow wanner watch yourselves. This is the wussest bit of the cut. An' they doh do nuthin abaht it neither, bloody BCN. Yow know what BCN stands for? Birmingham Canals Neglect. They'm bloody useless.'

This made me pretty anxious and I wondered who these bandits were. There was nothing in the guide-books about Mexicans. But John had something else on his mind.

'Where are you going with that thing?' John asked, pointedly ignoring me and the ominous warning, as he is wont to do when he is more curious than cautious.

'I'm tekking it back to Brierley 'Ill,' was the haughty reply, as if it was obvious to anyone but an imbecile. 'Ownly it's my new boat. Oi've just gorrit.'

'You live in a boat?' I asked, temporarily forgetting my fear and joining the curiosity brigade.

'Ar, 'ave done for years,' our new friend explained. 'Used to be a fire-fighter till I retired. Then I bought the boat. Once yow've lived on a boat, yow'll never goo back to brick.'

There's not a lot you can say to that. Fortunately, while we were still working on an appropriately witty response, another bloke arrived on a well worn mountain bike. He was a bit older and quite a bit chubbier, which was why the colour was high in his cheeks and he was breathing hard. However, he hadn't got the spray-on mud splashes like his Stourbridge counterparts of our first day.

'I've just seed three of the buggers up theer on the bridge,' he began, gulping for breath. 'I told 'em to clear off and, when they said "Who's gunner mek we?", I showed 'em me windlass and that scared 'em off.'

What was a mountain biker doing with a windlass, I wondered. This was getting more ominous by the minute.

'See whot I mean?' said the tall bloke. 'Bandit Country. Doh say I day warn yow.'

But he could sense we wanted to get on and he turned back to his boat, while we - me apprehensively, John brazenly - moved alongside the first lock where the middle-aged couple's narrowboat was just bobbing up above the lock walls.

'Gee, isn't the physics just wonderful?' shouted out the man in this boat in an American accent.

Can you imagine anyone other than an American saying that? I mean, it would be hard enough to find anyone in Britain who *thought* physics was wonderful, let alone had the courage to shout it out loud to a couple of strangers. And in Bandit Country too!

He was a bit older than we had at first thought, tall and bearded, and clearly enjoying himself but, on closer inspection, his boatmanship didn't live up to his confident words.

'Hey, it would be real nice if you could help us through these locks. I don't really want any unpleasantness,' he added.

Now real Americans are not supposed to sound like this, are they? They're supposed to be really gung-ho, up-and-at-em types, their guns primed to ward off any unwelcome strangers. I expect Americans faced with the threat of intruders immediately to transmute themselves into the Lone Ranger or the Cisco Kid and to take on these scummy bandits. Then, having clearly outfought them with their six-shooters as their horses whinny in the clouds of dust they have created, to chase them back across the border whence they came (in this case, Great Bridge).

This American was defying my stereotypes. But John and I are such naturally helpful people that next minute there we were, opening lock gate paddles with the windlass, leaning our backsides on the balance beams to close the heavy gates behind the boat as it chugged on to the next lock, and generally behaving as if we had spent our lives on cuts. We could even have corralled one of the Black Country 'osses and let it take the strain, while we stood on deck in our flat caps and scarlet neckerchiefs, sipping tea from a metal jug painted with brightly-painted roses and castles. What a life, eh!

But it was not to last. At the eighth lock, John nipped up to a nearby pub, appropriately called The Eight Locks (lots of imagination in use when these places were built) to use the toilet.

During his absence, I whiled away the time talking to a bloke in a blue boiler suit who was sat on the beam of the top lock eating strawberries. I asked him about this Bandit Country business and he said that he didn't know about that, though he wouldn't be surprised because it was a bit rough around there. Apparently, there is a dredger boat that comes up the cut from Birmingham twice a week, clearing out any rubbish. The local citizens know what days this boat comes and chuck their dead fridges, bicycles, prams, televisions, grannies and so forth over the fence and into the cut just before it gets there.

'Okay?' I asked John as he rejoined me.

'Just about', he said. 'There was this twenty-stone tattooed local at the bar. "Wor yow on the telly?" he wanted to know. But I didn't like the look on his face so I didn't stop to answer him. I ran out of the back door.'

We didn't wait to see if he had been followed. We increased our speed quite a bit and, with fear in our tread, set course for Smethwick.

Just then, the wife of the American boater, with whom we had been operating the locks for the past half an hour or so and with whom we had naturally been engaging in conversation about their trip (by boat to Birmingham) and our trip (by foot to Smethwick), came rushing up to press £5 into my hand.

'It's for your sponsorship,' she explained. 'We're really grateful for your help.'

'But there weren't any bandits,' I protested. 'Anybody could have done what we did. Really you shouldn't.'

But she insisted and I have to say I was slightly flattered that I should be taken as someone who might scare off bandits in Great Bridge. And, not only that, but actually be paid for it.

If only the Tipton Slasher could see me now!

The next stretch of our walk has to be one of the busiest bits of transport engineering anywhere in the world. New York city, eat your heart out! From Ryders Green Junction we ignored the Ridgeacre Branch, that goes to a dead end in West Bromwich, and followed the line of what had now become the Wednesbury Old Canal up to its junction with the good old BCN. Here we rejoined Telford's new route as it runs in parallel with the original Brindley cut into Smethwick. Telford's chosen route runs spectacularly through a steep-sided forty-foot deep cutting where the first flowers of spring – daffodils and primroses – were clustered decoratively. Above us to our left was the main West Coast railway line and beyond that we could see the pale concrete stilts that carry the M5 motorway through the Black Country. The cut weaves its way under, alongside and through these various transportation routes. Some spectacular bridges are evident here – the motorway stilting itself, the Telford Aqueduct that takes a short stretch from the old Brindley line over the newer line, the impressive Galton Bridge with its one hundred and fifty-feet cast iron span, and the Steward Aqueduct where the old line crosses the new line parallel to the motorway.

For the first time on our trek, however, and not unexpectedly given our stopovers in Willenhall and Wednesbury, we were rather pressed for time. So, when we reached Smethwick town itself with the magnificent Sikh temple glowing in the late afternoon sun, we did not stop but continued for a further half mile or so along the towpath because of an appointment we had. I had found out previously that the site of the Soho Foundry, widely acknowledged as one of the most significant in the history of the Industrial Revolution, was not open to the public but that a small museum on the site could be visited by prior appointment. I had duly written to make such an appointment (this all sounds a bit like James Boswell preparing the way for Dr. Johnson, doesn't it?) and had agreed a late afternoon time for our visit.

The Soho Foundry, where James Watt and Matthew Boulton opened the world's first engineering works in 1796, still occupies the same grounds, though the buildings have changed considerably. The site was acquired by the weighing machine manufacturers Avery towards the end of the nineteenth century and it is still owned by that company, now known as Avery Berkel. Mike Cooper of Avery Berkel gave us a very helpful tour of the grounds. We were shown the old Foundry building itself, now little more than a shell and crying out for some enterprising arm of government, local or national, to convert it into a working museum. It was here that Watt's invention of a separate condenser allowing steam power to be efficiently and effectively harnessed in order to drive machines was used by the organisational genius of Matthew Boulton to create the world's first manufacturing works. And what were they making? Why, steam engines, of course. Steam engines that went around the world and revolutionised the way people lived. Steam engines that transformed a world of cottage industries into one of factory production.

We also visited the building that housed the Mint and then the cottage once occupied by Boulton's and Watt's first Foundry Manager, the Scot William Murdock, who also happened to be the inventor of gas lighting. This led me to consider - "How would you invent gas lighting?"

Well, in Oor Wullie's case he was sitting around in some tin mines in Cornwall trying to do *The Scotsman* crossword by candlelight when he had a brainwave.

'Jings!' he thought. 'If ah invented gas lightin', I wouldnae hae to nip doon to the Spar shop for new candles ivry day. An', with the time that I've saved, I might even finish *The Scotsman* crossword.'

And that's the true story of the invention of gas lighting.

The museum that we were taken to has only a few artefacts from the Boulton and Watt era but it is of special interest and importance in itself. So, as well as the marble bust of James Watt, a copy of the deed of sale of the foundry to Avery's, dies used to mint coins, and rifles believed to have been used for protection during the Priestley Riots, it houses a wonderful collection of weighing machines. Now, you're probably thinking, as I did when I first heard about this, that there would be nothing but row after row of those things they used to have on railway stations to occupy children's time while waiting for trains. But no, it's a lot more than that. And a lot more remarkable than that.

'Weighing is at the heart of all human dealings,' explained Mike. 'And probably always has been.'

And, by way of clarification, he showed us some of the artefacts that have been collected over the years from different countries and different historical periods.

'Ever since humans began to trade,' Mike said, 'they have needed accuracy in weighing whatever they are trading in.'

And when you think about it, it's true, isn't it? So there are such exhibits as apothecary's scales for weighing tiny amounts of drugs and powders, huge machines for weighing metal girders, and scales for weighing jockeys before and after races. It was all quite fascinating.

The Soho Foundry site is surrounded by old brick walls topped with coils of menacing barbed wire. The area is still largely devoted to manufacturing, with a number of light engineering and motor component factories and an increasing number of clothing manufacturers, usually with Indian or Pakistani ownership, making leisurewear and other goods. In one sense, cottage industry has returned to the Black Country.

But we had had a long day and we were feeling a little jaded. Our guest house for the night was, unfortunately, some distance away and I could sense that John was not keen to walk there.

'Let's get a taxi,' he suggested. 'We've done our proper walk for the day. We don't have to be martyrs, do we?'

Once again, purely in the interests of sociability, I concurred and we rang for a taxi from the site of the Soho Foundry, surely one of the most important sites in the creation of our world. Without what happened here from 1795 onwards, we would have had to walk to our night's rest.

I used the £5 the American woman had given me to pay for the taxi. Well, she wasn't an official sponsor. And who would ever know anyway?

TWENTY TWO

SEEKING SIKHS IN SMETHWICK

When I was doing the reconnoitring for our journey, I had called in at Smethwick Library to enquire about possible accommodation.

'You need the Housing Department,' I was told.

'No, no,' I explained hastily. 'I only want accommodation for one night. I'm doing a walk around the cuts.'

The woman looked at me askance.

'You don't want to stay round here,' she said, lowering her voice so no one else could hear. 'It's not very nice.'

Now, I *think* she meant that Smethwick town is a very deprived area, which it is, but I suspect she meant something else as well. For, Smethwick, or Smevvick as it's usually pronounced locally, has a long and unfortunate association with racism. During the nineteen-twenties its M.P. was Oswald Mosley, then a member of the Labour Party but, of course, later to be the leader of the British Union of Fascists, a.k.a. the Blackshirts. Later, having attracted large numbers of Afro-Caribbean and Asian incomers during the post-war period because of its high employment opportunities in metal-bashing of one sort or another, Smethwick was home to the Conservative M.P. Peter Griffiths, who stood for election in 1966 on the platform of "If you want a nigger neighbour, vote Labour". So you can see why I was doubtful, even though I'd been led to believe that Smethwick had changed a lot.

Anyway, even after her colleagues had been consulted, it appeared there wasn't any accommodation of the sort we wanted in the centre of Smethwick. The imposing Blue Gates Hotel standing next to the library is apparently just a public house, though licensed premises have existed on that site for over two hundred years and it has served as a hotel in the past. The closest I could find was the Dinara Hotel out on the road towards Birmingham so that's where we were taken in our taxi.

Our host at the Dinara was called Jorvan. From his accent it was clear he was not from the Black Country. The hotel lounge is decorated with large pictures of men in walrus moustaches from a different age, some in military uniforms of great colour. I assumed they had something to do with where Jorvan came from.

So I asked Jorvan where his homeland was.

'I come from the country that once was Yugoslavia. Today it's called Croatia,' he replied. 'Tomorrow?'

And he shrugged his shoulders. But, no matter how hard we tried to get him to tell us more about his background, Jorvan would say nothing more so there is a mystery there that I would have dearly liked to solve but was unable to. I spent a little time looking again at the pictures but was no clearer than before. So I tried to put the whole thing out of my mind as our second appointment of the day was close at hand and we still had to wash and change, ready for our evening out.

I've already mentioned the Sikh Temple in Smethwick High Street. Originally a mid-nineteenth century Congregationalist church, it was acquired in the nineteen-sixties by the Sikh community in Smethwick. They converted it into the Guru Nanak Gurdwara Temple. At the time of its opening it was the largest Sikh temple outside India and over the years it has become the most splendid edifice in the town. Neither John nor I had ever been into a Sikh Temple, so I had arranged for an old friend of mine, a Sikh named Ajit Sahota with whom I had once worked, to collect us and take us into the gurdwara.

Ajit appeared at seven that evening and drove us into Smethwick High Street, stopping outside the gurdwara.

'What do you have to do to be a Sikh?' asked John, gazing at the temple.

'If you are a good human being,' Ajit replied simply, 'you are a good Sikh.'

That shut John up long enough for Ajit to give us a brief explanation of Sikhism and of what we would see inside and how we should behave.

As we sat in his car in Smethwick High Street, listening to his explanations, we watched a number of Sikhs entering the building. And soon we joined them, removing our shoes and putting scarves over our heads in the outer lobby area before moving into the main hall of the gurdwara. At the front sat the priest and beside him, cross-legged on the floor, were three singers and musicians performing some dreamlike chants. We sat at the back against a wall, watching entranced. Men and women, young and old, entered the temple and one by one made their obeisance to the Guru Granth Sahib before taking their places on the floor at their respective sides of the room.

An air of calm and peace filled our minds and hearts as we watched and listened. It was an uplifting experience and one that gives the lie to all those racists who think that people originally from the Asian subcontinent are beggars or scroungers. Sikhs have suffered huge discrimination against them since they settled in the United Kingdom, largely because of the badges of their culture that distinguish them and notable among those badges is the turban worn to keep their uncut hair under control. Ajit himself, before he came to live in England, had been a senior lecturer in a teacher training college but could not work in our state education system because he insisted on wearing a turban. The only work he could get was physical labouring in a foundry.

All these sombre thoughts were coursing through my brain as we took in the service we had been so graciously received into. No one gave us a second glance, other than smiles of welcome, and no one made us feel uncomfortable.

As we left the building, Ajit realised that we had left our shoes in the women's part of the lobby area, a fact which gave great amusement to three older Sikh women who shared John's big grins when this was pointed out.

The way we were treated did much to restore my faith in people's ability to live together harmoniously.

'That was magic,' said John, as we stood outside in the dusk of the evening.

And it was.

Having persuaded Ajit to introduce us to Sikhism and the Smethwick gurdwara, we then convinced him to take us to a pub in West Bromwich called The Vine for our evening meal. Now The Vine is an example of all that's good in the Black Country. It has an Asian landlord, whose photograph adorns the wall behind the bar. He is wearing that traditional costume of his Indian ancestors – the kilt! The barmaid, who has one of the biggest smiles I have ever seen in my life, is Afro-Caribbean. The kitchen staff are all white and work incredibly hard and incredibly politely. The clientèle is cosmopolitan and from every generation. Nowhere else in our travels did we see so many people of differing cultures, colours and origins living naturally side by side, and clearly enjoying each other's company and the comfort of being part of such a warm, vibrant, multi-racial community.

For the third night in a row I ordered a curry, this time a methi chicken massala, with poppadums and chips. All washed down with

Banks's bitter. How's that for multi-culturalism? John and Ajit ordered similar meals and the whole lot came to about a tenner. What value! And what flavours!

Afterwards, I asked Ajit to drive us to Bishop Asbury's cottage, not because it's anything special in itself but because it was the childhood home of Francis Asbury, who rose from being an apprentice blacksmith to be the founder of the Methodist church in America. This was in the latter half of the eighteenth century, at the time when the first cuts were being built and when Bilston enamels were having their moment in the sun. Asbury came from a religious family and became a Methodist after attending a service in Wednesbury where John Wesley had been persecuted some years earlier. Asbury became a local preacher at the age of eighteen and then, after giving up his job as a smith, travelled around the middle of England preaching. At the age of twenty-six he answered Wesley's call for volunteers to go to America and landed in Philadelphia in 1771. For almost fifty years he travelled extensively throughout America, following the earliest pioneers as they moved west. His travels and the hardships he endured are the stuff of legend but his achievement was to establish the Methodist church in America, at a time when it was breaking free of British rule. During his lifetime, the church grew from about one thousand to two hundred thousand members. Bishop Asbury is, in many ways, West Bromwich's most famous son.

One place we couldn't visit, because it no longer exists, is the small factory where Robert Spear Hudson, a chemist by training, invented and manufactured dry soap powder. His factory operated in West Bromwich for some years before he moved to larger premises in Liverpool which were later taken over by Lever Brothers. Now if you are one of that third of the population that regularly watches *Coronation Street* or *Eastenders*, or that smaller proportion that can't get by without

Neighbours or *Home and Away*, or even if you're one of those sad people who spend their life moaning about how there's too many soaps on the television when you would rather be watching football, then you'll appreciate why Robert Spear Hudson matters. Because it was in order to sell soap powders that the whole notion of a soap opera came about in nineteen thirties America. The idea was to capture radio listeners' attention by a family-based storyline in order to advertise your soap powder to them. And just look at how well they've succeeded.

And that's all down to West Bromwich.

TWENTY FOUR

BOING BOING, WEST BROM

Generally speaking, the cut builders did what most sensible people do and avoided the centre of West Bromwich. The Tame Valley cut goes to the north of it and the good old BCN stays south. And West Bromwich didn't have its own Earl of Dudley wanting to get a share of the action by digging his own link between the two. So, we had to invent an excuse for visiting West Bromwich on our journey and that excuse was the need to eat.

No one really knows why West Bromwich is called what it is. Until the nineteenth century it was believed that it did not exist as such until the thirteenth or fourteenth centuries. Then an enterprising local historian found a place called Bromwic in Northamptonshire in William the Conqueror's Domesday Book and saw that Northamptonshire belonged to William Fitz Ansculf, whose castle was in Dudley, and realised that there had been, literally, a clerical balls-up in the said Domesday Book. And, yes, Bromwic, it turned out, was where present-day West Bromwich is situated, not in Northamptonshire at all.

Lucky, eh?

But, why *West* Bromwich? And when *West* Bromwich?

That's what no one knows. There are two widely-held theories which prevail. One is that it was so called because it was west of Birmingham and took its name from there. But this brings forth two objections. First, as is obvious to anyone with basic map-reading skills, it is more north than west of the second city. Secondly, the root of Birmingham is believed to be Birming, son of Birm, not Brom meaning Broom, which is definitely the root of Bromwich. The other idea is that

174

it gained the West in order to distinguish it from Castle Bromwich and Little Bromwich, now absorbed within Birmingham. But then why not Big Bromwich? Or Upper Bromwich? Or Bostin' Bromwich?

It's another of those puzzles that the Black Country is so full of.

West Bromwich's Official Guidebook used to carry a description of the town that drew marked comparisons with Chicago, presumably because of the similarity of their manufacturing bases. It made us look carefully at everyone we passed on the High Street, wondering which of them were gangsters. It was hard to tell in the half-light but there were some rather suspicious-looking coats and hats and John didn't fancy taking his next trip to the cut in a concrete overcoat. In reality, I fear the main gangsters in West Bromwich nowadays are the gangsta rappers whose posters are plastered on every vacant space along the long High Street, which used to be known as the Golden Mile for some unfathomable reason.

Now, West Bromwich's problem is that the people in the other constituent towns of Sandwell, that is Wednesbury, Tipton, Rowley Regis, Oldbury and Smethwick, all believe that West Bromwich got all the goodies out of the local government reorganisation which created Sandwell in the first place in 1974. You only have to go into West Bromwich's main shopping centre on a weekday morning to see that's demonstrably not true. It's just another little Black Country town. It's not Wolverhampton. It's not Walsall. In fact, it's not even Dudley. It's no wonder that those who can afford it go to Merry Hill. Even Asda at Great Bridge has got more going for it.

It's a shame, really. The High Street, which was the main shopping centre before shopping centres as such became all the rage, was split in two some years ago in order to create another of those racetracks for boy racers that councils seem so keen on providing. Nowadays the only way to get from one side of the High Street to the other is to risk life and limb by dodging through the traffic that's hell-bent on mowing you down, or to go through the urine-smelling and chip-paper-filled underpasses.

One thing that West Bromwich does have, however, apart from the Baggies, who we'll come to in a while, is the best named fish and chip shop in the Black Country. This is a personal view, of course, but it comes after extensive field research (undertaken while the food police were busy at training camp). Chip shops seem to choose one of two styles for their names. They either go for the exotic-sounding, usually with some hint of a romantic source for their fish, like the Atlantis Fish Bar in Wolverhampton, the Blue Oyster Fish Bar in Old Hill, the Miami Fish Bar in Bilston, the Ocean Fish Bar in West Bromwich, the Palm Beach Fish Bar in Walsall, or the Zorba Fish Bar in Stourbridge. Or they go for punning, such as in the Frying Scotsman in Tipton, Hooked on Fish in Cradley Heath, the Keen Fryer in Brierley Hill, Our Plaice Too in Quarry Bank, or The Tasty Plaice in Oldbury.

But the best of the lot, near the centre of West Bromwich, is called Chip 'N' Deli.

Mind you, the very best fish and chip shop name I've ever seen was somewhere in Stoke-on-Trent. This was The Codfather! Now, if some enterprising West Bromwich chippie had called itself that, then it could truly compare itself to Chicago.

This brings me to the bit I've been trying to avoid for too long – the real reason for the continued existence of West Bromwich. This is in order to justify its football team, West Bromwich Albion, a.k.a. The Throstles, a.k.a. The Baggies, a.k.a., if you grew up like I did in Wolverhampton, The Enemy.

Now, I'm going to be completely objective in this section because it is not my intention to cause offence to anyone who supports West Brom. However, I cannot avoid clarifying for readers beyond the Black Country some of the most frequently asked questions about the club.

First of all, then, the reason why they are known as The Throstles is because, after playing in a variety of grounds in the early part of their life, the club moved to its present ground, The Hawthorns, in 1900. The ground then was largely common land with many hawthorn bushes that attracted large numbers of song-thrushes, otherwise known as throstles. So that soubriquet is easily explained. Until, that is, you look at the club's badge and see this bird, which might just pass for a thrush, sitting on a branch of what looks like a raspberry bush. So were there really raspberry bushes in West Bromwich in 1900? Or was the artist who designed this badge some kind of nutter? Or is this just another example of the kind of blindness to reality that afflicts so many Baggies fans?

And why The Baggies? This is a bigger mystery and we need the help of official publications for some of the possibilities.

·It is a corruption of "Magee", who was a popular full back in the nineteen-twenties.

·It is from the name of protective trousers that factory workers in the area used to wear.

·It originates with supporters who took bags (baggies) round to local pubs to save the club from extinction in 1905.

·When the club was nearly bankrupt in the nineteen-hundreds, a number of the larger players left. Their shoes and the rest of their kit was passed on to smaller players. Spotting their voluminos shorts, a wag in the crowd is supposed to have shouted "Up the Baggies".

·Another version is that the club used to have a big full-back called Amos Adams whose thick hips made his baggy pants look even bigger. One match, when he was not playing well, a fan shouted "Baggy" and the name stuck.

Now, as if that wasn't confusing enough, the current logo used in marketing West Bromwich Albion football club is "Boing Boing Baggies". Why is this? It's because at a match in recent years (there's the inevitable dispute about which match and which season and who saw it first) some fans started jumping up and down and waving their arms about, like jack-in-the boxes. Whether they did this because it was cold or because they were bored or simply because this is the sort of lunatic behaviour that you might expect from anyone who has been blessed with the affliction of being a Baggies supporter, I do not know. But, it is true, so I am told on the highest authority, i.e. *Grorty Dick*, the Albion fanzine published by (wouldn't you just know?) Dick Publications. There's even a bunch of sad lads who belong to a team called Boing F.C.

Grorty Dick and all its works are, of course, the unofficial face of West Bromwich Albion. It's only fair to put the more official line on the club. Perhaps you might get a sense of this if I tell you that, from the official West Bromwich Albion shop, you can purchase items such as fridge magnets, bum bags, car care kits, millennium mouse mats and children's Albion woolly gloves, all tastefully embellished with the club's badge and motto. For the real aficionado with the finest of taste there is a complete bedroom set, comprising curtains, duvet set, wallpaper and border strip, and a framed wall clock. How can you not buy this?

What else can I tell you about West Bromwich Albion? Well, their ground at The Hawthorns is the highest in Britain, being some five hundred and fifty feet above sea level, though it's probably the ground that's farthest from the sea as well. And it seats some 25, 296 fans. And the pitch size is 115 yards by 75 yards. And the club was one of the founder members of the Football League in 1888. And recently their supporters were voted the worst-dressed fans in the world, possibly because of those protective trousers that they all wear. Their response to this was pathetic – they all dressed up in borrowed monkey suits for the last match of the season. Who did they think they were kidding?

There's not much to tell you about the footballing side of things. Like their arch-rivals, Wolves, the Albion have seen better days. They last won the League in 1920 and their best years were in the nineteen fifties, when they won the F.A. Cup and finished second in the League (to the Wolves, ha ha!). At the end of the 1999-2000 season they narrowly missed being relegated to the Second Division. They tend to change managers every few months and the opinion of the three men in the Old Blue Ball, Wednesbury, when we were eating our sandwiches there on the fourth day of our expedition, is probably the most appropriate to the club's current standing. So, to save you looking back, I'll repeat it.

'They wus crap.'

And that's all I have to say about West Bromwich and its football team.

TWENTY FOUR

IT'S A LONG WAY TO OLDBURY

You will find this hard to believe but, when we woke up on the final morning of our trip, the sun was shining. It was difficult to remember that only three days previously we had been struggling through slush and sleet as we left Tipton. But there it was. Global warming? Chernobyl? Sellafield? Who knows what the cause of this turbulent weather is. Or maybe it's just the sort of mixed up April that even Geoffrey Chaucer's pilgrims would have recognised as they wended their way to Canterbury all those many years ago.

Jorvan's breakfast was not as large as some of those we had endured but it was the usual cholesterol special. We lingered over it fondly, knowing that this was our last opportunity for a while to escape from the muesli and wholemeal toast regimes that the food police at home would reimpose upon us. I tried again to get Jorvan to talk about the pictures on the wall but all he would say was that some of them were very old before he scuttled off to the kitchen for some more toast.

So we packed our bags one final time and, leaving them at the Dinara for my wife to collect later in the day, set off back into Smethwick town centre and thence over the Tollhouse Way footbridge with its splendid views of the history of land transportation. Crossing this bridge, you can see the High Street and a modern dual carriageway, the electrified West Coast railway line, and the Old Line of the BCN cut, originally built by Brindley, twenty feet higher than Telford's New Line cut visible below it. Our route was along the Old Line that quickly took us away from the noise of traffic and the bustle of the town. Soon we were on top of one of those wonders of early engineering, the Steward Aqueduct that Telford built to enable the Old Line to cross his New Line in 1828. Now I know I've commented about Thomas T. before but I do have to say that, brilliant engineer and all-round brainbox that he was, he was also a bit of an arrogant so-and-so. Cast your eyes over this from the report on the Smethwick stretch he wrote for the BCN when they asked him in the eighteen-twenties to look at ways of improving Brindley's original cutting.

"I found adjacent to this great and flourishing town a canal a little better than a crooked ditch with scarcely the appearance of a towing path, the horses frequently sliding and staggering in the water, the hauling lines sweeping gravel into the canal and the entanglement at the meeting of the boats incessant; while at the locks at each end of the short summit, crowds of boatmen were always quarrelling…and the mineowners, injured by the delay, were loud in their just complaints."

That's one way to get yourself a job, eh?

But even Thomas T. couldn't have foreseen what we were now experiencing, for the Old Line of the BCN that we were following runs directly underneath and parallel to the M5 motorway. It was a weird feeling to be walking steadily along the towpath with no one else in sight, yet knowing that high above us thousands of people were speeding north or south on the stilted motorway oblivious of us. At one point we became aware of CCTV cameras attached to some of the concrete stanchions supporting the motorway and could only surmise that they were there to deter youngsters from climbing up to the road. Was this some form of 'chicken' practised here? There was no one to ask and no one to tell.

Many of the features of the cut on this stretch, like bridges and the towpath itself, were rebuilt at the time when the motorway was being created, so it came as a bit of a shock to find an old bridge called Blakeley Hall Bridge. Now, not many people know this but Blakeley Hall was a stately home in this part of the Black Country, on the borders between Smethwick and Oldbury. It was built in the late sixteenth century for a certain William Birkdale, a gentleman at court, whose family lived there for many years until it was the victim of fire in the early nineteenth century. It is said that Blakeley Hall was the original home of Mr Bingley that Jane Austen was thinking of when she had Mrs Bennett report the news that he, Bingley, was coming to Hertfordshire, and that he must be in want of a wife.

Now, if you believe that, you'll believe anything. It is, of course, a complete fabrication, invented for your delight. And yet, presumably there was a real Blakeley Hall somewhere near this mass of road and rail and cut in what is now the Black Country. And presumably somebody rich lived in it. But how would we know? That's why we need some signage. Even if no one knows anything about Blakeley Hall, I'm sure someone knows about the number of men and days and spades it took to build this cut or the number of vehicles travelling daily on that motorway or the speed of the intercity trains on that railway. And wouldn't a few judicious signs giving that information help to make the journey a little more interesting?

I'm even prepared to sell the authentic documents that prove my story of Blakeley Hall to an appropriate body. Offers in writing please.

The New Line of the BCN, which we were not following, goes virtually straight from Smethwick through to Wolverhampton and runs very close to a station on the main West Coast railway line which is known as Sandwell and Dudley station. This has always struck everyone in the Black Country as daft, because it's four miles away from Dudley and because Sandwell, as I've already explained, doesn't exist as such. It is actually Oldbury Station but it was rechristened in order to appease the powers-that-be of these two neighbouring councils.

And that's where the funny part of this comes in. You see, British Rail, having demolished the old wooden-floored station and replaced it with a two million quid concrete platform, decided they ought to have a proper opening ceremony. So, all the civic dignitaries from Sandwell and all the civic dignitaries from Dudley, the mayors and their corporations no less, were invited to this launch. So, there they all were in their best togs on the platform waiting for the first train to stop there. Unfortunately, the first train to come through did not stop. Somebody had forgotten to tell the driver about this new station and the train sped through, leaving a trail of dust and a lot of surprised faces. However, the mayors and corporations were not to be cheated like that so various officials were detailed to organise another train. While they waited, someone had the bright idea to open the celebratory champagne and whisky laid on for the event. This was another mistake because it was quite some time before the next train was due and the alcohol coursing through the bladders of our civic representatives soon demanded release.

And, yes, that's right, there are no public lavatories at Sandwell and Dudley station.

When the second train did at last arrive, it was greeted with relief by a number of the assembled guests who gratefully scrambled aboard to use the facilities, ignoring the warnings within, forever immortalised in that well-known verse:

When the train is at the station
Please refrain from urination.

So, be warned if you ever have to disembark at Sandwell and Dudley station! It's nowhere near where you want to go and it's miles before you can have a pee.

The Old Line of the BCN creeps round the town of Oldbury, so we climbed off the towpath at Seven Stars Bridge and braved the ring road to get to the town centre. Oldbury used to be known as "The Town of the Four Moons" because the light from four of the hundred or so blast furnaces within the town's boundaries was so bright that the authorities delayed providing gas lighting for many years in the early nineteenth century.

You'll gather from this that Oldbury has been a centre of manufacturing for a long time. There is a legend told about a pre-war expedition to New Guinea that discovered over a ridge of mountains a tribe of people who had never had any contact with the world beyond the hills that surrounded their valley. These people thought they were the only people that existed but they had one proud possession – a hunting knife made in Oldbury. No one knows how it got there.

Whatever the truth of that, there is no doubt that there were forges operating in Oldbury from the early seventeenth century onwards, making nails and other small items of ironware, but it was the opening of Brindley's cut that brought the great influx of industry to the town. Coal mines, blast furnaces and brickyards were followed by chemical works, like Albright and Wilson, and other industries. The place became synonymous with the Black Country at the heart of manufacture and of pollution. It never developed much in the way of civic buildings or shopping centres and that's probably why it was ripe for what has happened to it in the latter half of the twentieth century.

For Oldbury has been almost razed to the ground in order to create two huge ugly edifices – Savacentre and Sandwell Council House. The former is a huge Sainsbury's hypermarket selling food, clothing, household goods, toys and electrical products. It claims to offer sixty two thousand product lines of which about one third are food and grocery products. Last year, among other significant offerings to the gentle burghers of Oldbury, the good lords of Sainsbury introduced a range of French patisseries, selected co-ordinates for adults and children and the popular Mr Men on selected childrenswear. Wasn't that jolly decent of them?

Sandwell Council House is known as The Kremlin. It sits squat in the middle of Oldbury and, like its Moscow counterpart, administers its territory with socialist fervour. Sandwell has always been a Labour-led authority, as it was when it comprised the separate authorities of West Bromwich and Warley. The council is the biggest employer in Sandwell and large numbers of those employees are sucked into The Kremlin daily at about nine in the morning and disgorged later at about five o'clock in the afternoon. Some lucky ones are allowed out at lunchtime. On a fine day, you can see them wondering around the empty town of Oldbury in their Ciro Citterio suits, blinking in the sunlight, looking for somewhere to buy sustenance. Usually they end up purchasing a sandwich in Savacentre, in whose monstrous shell they feel safe again, before they scurry back to their desks in The Kremlin.

Those council workers have probably never noticed the wooden bench that sits among some flower beds in front of the war memorial in a desolate patch at the side of Savacentre. And, even if they were to notice it, they probably would not appreciate its significance. A small bronze plaque on this bench bears the following inscription:

JACK JUDGE

AUTHOR AND COMPOSER OF TIPPERARY

A SONG THAT UPLIFTED THE HEART AND SPIRIT

OF THOSE WHO SAW ACTIVE SERVICE IN TWO WORLD WARS

Jack Judge came from Oldbury and lived in that part of town that was demolished in the nineteen sixties to make way for the ring road, Savacentre and Sandwell Council House.

'Apparently, he was a fishmonger by trade,' I told John, 'but he entertained in the music halls at night.'

'Sounds a bit like how I got started,' he replied. 'I was a telephone engineer originally but I used to perform at night time.'

Jack Judge's main claim to fame is the composition of *It's a Long Way to Tipperary*, which he wrote in a few hours to win a five shilling bet with one of his fellow-performers in a musical show. This fellow-performer was a seal trainer and, when Jack Judge gave his first performance of Tipperary at a music hall in Stalybridge, Cheshire, he was accompanied by the performing seals – an inauspicious beginning.

The song became associated with the First World War almost by accident. Jack Judge was performing in a pantomime in Dublin during the winter of 1913-14 in which he sang *Tipperary* and there received a visit from a battalion of the Connaught Rangers who had come specially from their winter quarters in Tipperary to hear him sing the song. Six months later Archduke Ferdinand was assassinated in Sarajevo, precipitating the First World War, and a few days after that the same battalion of Connaught Rangers disembarked in Boulogne, ready for action. As they came jauntily down the gang-plank, they broke into a spontaneous chorus of *It's a Long way to Tipperary*, which happened to be witnessed by the Daily Mail's war correspondent. His report was passed to all allied and American newspapers and, from that moment on, Jack Judge's song was inextricably linked with the war in the public perception. It was even used in Lord Kitchener's recruiting campaign and hundreds of thousands of young men marched off to their deaths singing this sentimental song by an Oldbury fishmonger.

Its nostalgic, easy-to-sing-along chorus still has the power to bring a lump to your throat. There's something in the range of the tune and something in the words that clutches at you and makes you pause and remember, almost more than you would the verses of Owen or Sassoon.

We sat on that bench and hummed the tune quietly to ourselves. And it worked.

Just shut your eyes and hum it to yourself.

See?

TWENTY FIVE

ANCHORED IN NETHERTON, MOORED IN OLD HILL

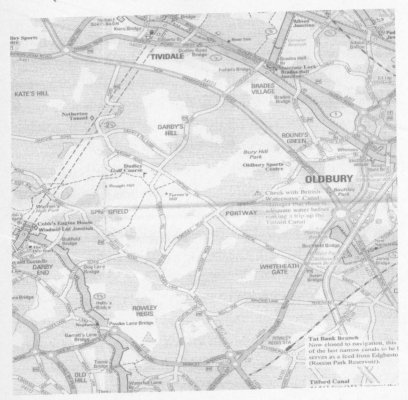

And so we marched along the towpath again, on the last lap of our journey. The sun was still shining as we strode purposefully along past the backs of pleasant housing estates and noisy factories, accompanied as ever by families of coots and moorhens. The aches and pains that had begun to be noticed the previous evening had disappeared now and there was a new jauntiness in our steps.

We were making good time again so, at Dudley Road West Bridge, I suggested we go in search of coffee. As luck would have it, just up the road from here is a caff which probably does merit the term of Greasy Spoon. The menu, handwritten on a board attached to the wall, promises sandwiches made with crusty bread containing bacon & egg for £1, bacon, egg & black pudding for £1.05, bacon, egg, sausage & black pudding for £1.10 and so on upwards to £1.25, with various combinations and extras. It's almost as complicated to work out as solving quadrilateral equations. There were three blokes smoking at one table and the only other person present, apart from us and the young woman who was serving, was an old crone who was wiping the tables with a mucky rag.

We sat down with our mugs of caffeine-flavoured water, stretched our legs and amused ourselves by trying to find combinations of food that were not on display and working out their price.

'The food 'ere is really bostin',' said the old crone, as she approached our table with her mucky rag. 'Specially the crusty bread.'

'Oh yes,' said John, ever eager to engage the natives in conversation. 'Why's that?'

Of course, that was just the invitation she had been angling for.

'A man loikes a proper crusty bread sandwidge,' she said, hands on hips. 'Summat 'e con get 'is 'onds rahnd.'

As they say, there's no answer to that. Even John was left speechless by this piece of profound Black Country philosophy. So we drained our cups and returned to the canalside, where very shortly we came to the reason why I had sought John's company in the first place – the two-mile unlit Netherton Tunnel which begins underneath the Old Line of the BCN in Tividale.

Netherton Tunnel was opened in 1858, having taken three years to build and costing nine men their lives and eighteen others serious injury during its construction. I was worried enough about going through this dark and dismal tunnel before I found that out - would their ghosts still be hovering in the gloom? This tunnel was built to relieve the pressure on the Dudley Tunnel, the "legging" tunnel of our first day's walk, which could not cope with the amount of canal traffic wanting to use it. Was our journey to see such activity? Would the towpath be overflowing with bandits? I was feeling real worry as we approached the entrance.

There a notice informed us that the first turf was cut by the Earl of Dudley (who else?). Of course, that settled my mind very well!

The tunnel is another remarkable piece of engineering. It is 2768 metres long, is wide enough for two boats to pass, and has a towpath on each side with iron railings, with passing places for horses. When it was opened it was lit by gas but this was replaced by electricity later. The gas and electric fittings are still visible inside the tunnel.

Visible, that is, if you have a torch, because once you leave the daylight all is gloom inside. And this is not helped by the optical illusion created by the visibility of the far end of the tunnel from the moment you enter. So you go from pleasant surprise at thinking it's not that far really through mild irritation that it doesn't seem to be getting very much closer to total paranoia that you'll be destined to walk forever and never reach the end.

I had a torch, of course. I had read my guide to tunnels and come prepared. John, however, hadn't, so he had to trail along behind me, guessing at the path from the beam of my torch shining ahead of me. That was fine except when I did a sudden flick of the light on to the roof of the tunnel to point out a fascinating gas bracket to him or the dull glow from an upcoming shaft. And, although the tunnel is in a remarkably good state of repair since it was re-opened in 1984, its walls do have a tendency to leak. Consequently, there were a lot of quite deep puddles of water on the towpath and John went in most of them.

As it turned out, we didn't meet anyone walking through the tunnel, so John's skills as minder were not required. We were passed, however, by a boat going the opposite way, whose crew seemed particularly delighted to revisit their childhoods by shouting "Ooooooh" and "Aaaaaaah" into the echoing void. Maybe they *were* children, with very deep voices, for they passed us in the shadows and all we could hear were their voices.

Eventually, that hole at the other end became the exit from the tunnel and we came out into the bright sunshine and an area of former industrial land that has now become a nature reserve known as Warrens Hall Park. This looks like a moonscape, with its humpbacked pit mounds, its dips and its pools. Its major feature is the restored Cobb's Engine House, the last one of its kind left standing in the Black Country. In its day it was used to drain water from the mines of the local mineowner. It is made of bricks and stands ninety-five feet high. Next to it is an almost derelict building, part of the same complex originally, which once housed a smaller engine used to wind a lift up and down the mine shaft. This was shipped to the U.S.A. in 1928 by Henry Ford, who, for some strange reason, reassembled it in his museum in Dearborn, Detroit.

The names of two of the cut stretches around here are unusual - the Bumblehole Branch and the Boshboil Branch. They were once major thoroughfares but now are blocked off and serve only the glum fishermen. But another unusual name locally reveals a much more interesting story.

The Dry Dock Inn sits a short distance from the cut. Its bar is the hull of a salvaged boat set inside an imitation galleon. Its walls have a range of ornate and wacky decorations, such as tiles with pictures of pigs on them and watering cans painted with the roses and castles motif.

It used to have Irish Evenings, featuring local folksingers called Norfolk n' Good (think about it), and it sold a beer called Lumphammer and Desperate Dan Cow Pies. These latter comestibles were served in a large round dish, contained huge amounts of steak and vegetables in rich gravy, and were topped with a pastry lid punctured with two pastry horns. Those who managed to eat one of these monstrosities used to get a glutton's certificate.

You will gather from my description that this is how the Dry Dock *used* to be. It was one of a chain of pubs called the Little Pub Company set up by an Irish settler in the Black Country called Colm O'Rourke. The company's motto was "Where the Customer is Always Wrong" and its pubs were "dedicated to a decent pint, a plate of real wholesome food (none of your nevill cuisine in a pool of raspberry jam here!), good music, and of course the conversation and the crack". There was also Mad O'Rourke's Manic Pub Tour, whereby you could visit every one of the nineteen pubs in the chain over any period of time and, having got your passport stamped in each, be admitted to the Sacred Brotherhood of the Ancient and Noble Society of Little People.

Sadly, O'Rourke sold his chain of pubs some two years ago to Usher's brewery and things just are not the same nowadays. The Dry Dock still looks the same inside but the spirit has disappeared. Our pints of Usher's and our tuna sandwiches were quite acceptable but we were easily distracted by a pretty young woman sitting outside on the steps with two ugly-looking blokes. John suspected that they were drug dealers and that they used her as a front. I suspected she was a Romanian asylum seeker who had fallen in with some local louts and was being used by them as a prostitute. We whispered these thoughts to each other, however, not wishing to be overheard, because the two blokes didn't look as if they took prisoners.

As time moved on, more and more customers arrived, office workers mostly from a look at their clothes, encouraged out by the sunny weather. But we were not to be drawn into their casual chat about photocopiers and fans and fenestration, for our minds were on a higher plane. So we left.

After that brief, and I have to say somewhat disappointing, visit to the Dry Dock, which I had anticipated would make John jump up and down with glee, we returned to the towpath and followed it up into Netherton itself. There's not much to see in the town but it has three main claims to fame. It was once at the heart of the mining industry and there were inevitably a large number of ironworks that grew up alongside the mines. One of these was Noah Hingley's, which made anchors, chains, and chain cable for ocean-going liners, including the anchor for the infamous *Titanic*. One local wag says that the anchor was the only thing that worked on the ship! In the centre of Netherton there is a replica of this anchor, although you wouldn't know what it was unless you came from Netherton since there is no sign telling you what it is or what its significance was.

Another statue at the opposite end of this patch of ground that is little more than a traffic island in the middle of the town shows a squatting figure with weights attached to his downstretched arms. This, although again the lack of signage doesn't tell you, is a representation of Joe Darby who was world champion spring jumper in the latter years of the nineteenth century. You will never have heard of spring jumping because it is no longer practised, but neither was snowboarding or Scrabble-playing once. And, when you read of Joe Darby's feats, you might very well launch a campaign to introduce spring jumping into the Olympic Games in 2004.

Joe Darby performed his jumps in front of royalty and in matches for money. He could clear half a dozen chairs with a jump taken off an ordinary glass tumbler filled with water, without spilling a drop. He could jump over a full size billiard table lengthwise minus the cushions, taking off from a block of wood. And he could make a double spring on to the surface of water on and off again, wetting only the soles of his feet.

This last skill he demonstrated when he was a blacksmith by clearing the cut in two jumps, making the second leap from the surface of the water. Legend has it that he found this particularly useful if he ever needed to escape from the police. He was a remarkable man and he donated a collection of the trophies he won for his achievements to Dudley Museum before he died in 1936.

The third, and rather unusual, piece of Netherton's notoriety is that a factory called Barnsley's once produced all of the world's jews harps. The jews harp is a small metal instrument which is played by twanging it against the teeth. In 1935 Barnsley's was churning out these tiny instruments at a rate of one hundred thousand a week to meet the demand from all over the advanced world. For jews harps were the pogo sticks or the pokemon cards of their day and somebody had to make them, didn't they?

Back at the side of the cut just above the Dry Dock Inn occurred our one major trauma of the whole trip. There is a Visitors' Centre recently built there, which contains a variety of local maps and photographs and information about the area. It is staffed by volunteers and it was one of these who provided the excitement. He had spotted a youth on one of the nearby canal bridges carrying an air rifle and had challenged him to explain what he was doing with the gun.

'Shooting beer cans in the cut,' came the surly reply.

'No, yow wor,' said the ponytailed warden from the Visitors' Centre, who had now been joined by his female colleague and, I was horrified to see, by John. The three of them had surrounded the youth.

'I was.'

'Yow wor.'

'I was.'

'Yow wor.'

This went on for some time, with each statement gaining in emphasis and loudness as it became obvious that neither was prepared to give in.

'Where yow from then?' asked Ponytail, as if this would help the situation.

'From Waerles,' said the youth in a broad Black Country accent.

'Yow bay,' said the woman, whose florid expression suggested that she was about to launch herself at him. ' Doh yow worry, mate, the police am on theer way. Doh yow worry.'

'I doh care. They know me. Yow can axe them.'

'I can tek that gun off yow,' said Ponytail. 'Yow ay allowed to have it up 'ere. It's a nature reserve.'

'Yow cor tek it.'

'I can.'

'Yow cor.'

And so on.

There was then a brief tussle which resulted in Ponytail wresting the gun off the youth, who didn't put up much resistance to tell the truth. Probably because he saw the numbers stacked against him.

At this point John, ever the master of the *non sequitur*, decided it was his turn to join in.

'Why did you have that rifle then?' he asked.

I thought the youth was going to ask him if he'd once been famous, but no.

'I'm just looking after it for a mate,' said the youth.

'But why are you carrying a rifle over here?' John persisted. You can't beat John on logic.

'I wor gonna use it. I was just carrying it. Look, it's not cocked.'

Now Harold Pinter could have turned this dialogue into a West End play but I don't think I'm doing it its full justice so I will give you no more. All you need to know is that it carried on in this fashion for quite some time and was going nowhere, until I took out my camera to photograph Cobb's Engine House, whereupon the youth pulled his denim jacket over his face and took off at a rate of knots down the towpath. I presume he thought I was going to take a picture of him and give it to the coppers. There was no point in pursuit, so Ponytail, who held the air rifle proudly, thanked us for our help.

'We'm always getting 'is sort rahnd 'ere,' he said, then paused and looked quizzically at John. 'By the way, did yow used to be faermous?'

You see, even in Netherton where I once worked, it's John they remember, not me!

Now, although this little confrontation was won by the good guys, I have to say that I'm not sure it would have ended quite so happily if we had met this youth in the Netherton Tunnel. I silently thanked the heavens that I had asked John to accompany me. Who knows what difference a few hours and a few metres might have made? I might have been found floating on my back out of the tunnel in the wash of some canal boat and then you, dear reader, would have missed the pleasure of reading this book. Which, you will be sad to learn, is approaching its end.

For we now set off on the very last stretch of our journey following Dudley No.2 Canal around the base of the Rowley Hills and to its culmination at Gosty Hill Tunnel in Old Hill. This tunnel is impassable by foot and, although there is a footpath leading over the top of it and joining up with a final stretch of cut up to the edge of Halesowen, I had decided that Old Hill was to be our final stop, thus maintaining my original notion of walking around the Black Country.

We reached The Wharf Tavern there in the middle of the afternoon and enjoyed a final pint of beer as we awaited my wife, who was due to take us home after collecting our bags from the Dinara Hotel in Smethwick. While we sat in the garden of this pub, enjoying the brilliant hot sun, we were joined once again by Steve Clarke who had had guessed our arrival time and come to help us celebrate the completion of our fifty-mile trek. Steve is a native of Netherton and somewhere in the ensuing conversation he agreed to write a poem about the Black Country for my book. He produced it a few weeks later and it provides a fitting postscript to my narrative.

For, this was it. We had experienced rain, snow, cloud and sun. We had seen nuts and nutters, bugs and buggers, sortation centres and factory shells, art in galleries and art in public. We'd supped some of the Black Country's favourite beers, and eaten some of its favourite dishes. And we had done what we set out to do. We had completed our circuit of the Black Country without any further damage to my left knee or to John's back. In short, we had succeeded.

We were ready to go home.

TWENTY SIX

THE SPICE OF LYEFE

Mister Dave is an ex-disc jockey called David Homer who used to enjoy going to Balti restaurants in Birmingham fifteen or so years ago and noted all the Beamers, Rollers and Jags parked outside, despite the fact that in those days the restaurants were both cheap and cheap-looking. One day, on a fishing trip to Skegness with some mates, he suddenly announced that he was going to set up a Balti restaurant of his own in Lye. His mates all laughed and told him that only Indians could set up Indian restaurants but he insisted that he was going to do it himself and call it Mister Dave's. So he took himself off to one of the Birmingham Balti houses and got them to train him in Balti cooking, then he recruited a couple of staff from that restaurant and opened up. Within two weeks it was a resounding success. Within months two more Baltis had opened in Lye, which is a small town outside Stourbridge. There are now seven of them, including one amusingly named "The Spice of Lyefe". Sadly, Mister Dave's is no longer there because Dave Homer has moved very successfully into frozen Baltis and now prepares and sells twelve thousand meals a week under the distinctive Mister Dave logo.

So you think you know what a Balti is? But are you really sure?

As with so much else in the Black Country, there are two versions of the truth. Take your pick.

Here is the official version.

The Balti is a traditional dish which is very popular in the Northern Punjab and has its roots in Baltistan, now the northernmost part of Pakistan, which was once a kingdom with its own royals. Balti refers both to its area of origin and the dish in which the food is cooked and served on the table. The Balti pan is a round-bottomed, wok-like, cast-iron dish with two handles, which was originally brought from China along the ancient Silk Route, across the Karakoram Pass, through Baltistan and into the Punjab and then evolved into a slightly deeper, more rounded pan.

The dishes served in the Balti pan are freshly-cooked and aromatically-spiced curries. Balti food is very aromatic but not excessively spiked with chillies. Traditionally it is eaten without rice or cutlery. Balti bread is used to scoop up the food using the right hand. The origins of the Balti are wide ranging and owe as much to China and Tibet as to the tribal ancestry of the nomad, the tastes of the Moghul emperors, the aromatic spices of Kashmir, 'winter foods' of lands high in the mountains and the exotic flavours of Punjab.

The other version – and the one I subscribe to - is that it is a dish invented in Birmingham by some enterprising Pakistanis as a cheap meal for the early immigrants to this country.

Eight months after our epic walk and just as the year was turning, I persuaded John to join me for a Balti meal at The Spice of Lyefe. What better way to sum up a lifetime in the Black Country! I wanted to reflect, with his assistance, on our journey and what we had learned from it.

'The first thing is never to go walking with you again!' were his opening words after we'd ordered our Balti dishes and I'd told him of my purpose. 'At least, not unless you can pick a better time of the year. It's a wonder I didn't catch pneumonia.'

'Yes, but apart from that,' I pressed. 'What did you really think about it all?'

He munched thoughtfully on a poppadum before answering.

'Couldn't we just have gone to the Black Country Museum to see everything?' he said at length. 'It would have saved a lot of time.'

'No, I wanted to see the Black Country as it is, not just as it was, ' I retorted.

'True,' mused John. 'I don't remember too many flat caps and bicycles, although there was a lot more industry than I expected.'

'Yes, all the industrial stuff was interesting and it was important. But there was a lot more to it than that.'

'Like what?'

'It's difficult to say. After we got back and I started to write it all up, I became aware of this great sense of warmth running through me. I felt that, at long last, the Black Country had embraced me. Or maybe it was just me embracing and finally understanding the Black Country.'

'So what have you understood now that you didn't understand before?'

'I think it's just the vibrancy of the culture, ' I replied. '*You* know all about that, coming from Liverpool. Everybody has this notion of the strength of Scouse culture even when times are hard. That's why *Boys from the Black Stuff* was so powerful. I suppose I hadn't realised it was as powerful in the Black Country. Didn't you feel that?'

'Ye-es,' John said, a little hesitatingly. 'I have to say that some of the characters we met were amazing. I loved Rita in the caff. She was brilliant. She could have worked in any caff in Liverpool, if it wasn't for her accent.'

'I liked Jackie at the New Inn,' I mused, breaking another poppadum and spooning raita on to it. 'You missed all that stuff she told me about grey peas and bacon. It was fascinating.'

'So you keep saying,' he said, pulling a face. 'I've been back to that Art Gallery in Walsall, you know. Went for a day. It's even better than I remembered. Though I still don't like the building.'

'What about the Sikh Temple in Smethwick?'

'Yeah, that was brilliant too. But how can you summarise so much diversity?'

I sighed, as our waiter brought two steaming black bowls of Balti chicken and mushroom and a naan bread as big as your arm.

'I suppose,' I began, tearing off a chunk of naan bread to chew, 'it's the way that the Black Country just keeps adapting itself that strikes me most. It's always been an area of immigrants, right from the days of the early Saxon settlers, through the Norman invasion and then, when those Lunaticks started up the Industrial Revolution, it just soaked up newcomers from the counties round about and from Scotland, Ireland and Wales.'

'And now?' he quizzed. 'You kept talking about the racism in the Black Country and Enoch Powell and all that sort of thing. What d'you feel about all that now?'

'I really believe that Powell was wrong,' I said. 'Not just in the way he stirred up trouble but in his analysis of the population issue. The Black Country has always had to be driven by newcomers. It's always needed new blood to keep transforming it. Remember The Vine in West Bromwich? That pub we went into with Ajit?'

John nodded, chewing on a mouthful of Balti chicken thoughtfully.

'That's the reality of the Black Country,' I continued, waving a chunk of well-baked naan in his direction. 'That's where the future is being made, in places like that. I honestly believe that all those bigots who supported Enoch Powell - and I know there's still quite a few of them around - have had their day. Look at this place.'

I gestured around the room in The Spice of Lyefe, full of people of differing skin colour enjoying their Balti meals in the relaxed atmosphere of the sitar music quietly wafting through the air.

'Yes, but the sort of people you're talking about wouldn't come here,' John pointed out.

'More fool them,' I countered. 'Honestly, it's social Darwinism, isn't it? The social body has to adapt or die. And you know which I favour.'

John munched in silence, savouring the flavours of his Balti meal.

'Lye used to be the centre of the chain-making industry,' I explained further. 'Now it's the Balti capital of the Black Country. Brierley Hill used to be known for steel-making; now it's a shopper's paradise. They used to make motor bikes, cars and trolley buses in Wolverhampton; now its University is at the forefront of developments in computing. That's what the Black Country's all about. Adaptation. And besides.'

'What?' John asked, looking up as he heard my sigh.

'It's the people,' I said. 'They're just wonderfully warm. Despite the bad press, it's the people I love best. Captain Bob of the Dudley Tunnel boat, Rita and her clientèle in Perry's caff, Jackie of the New Inns, Mohammed in the Bilash, the old caps in The Tiger, Pauline and Mike at the Acacia (or is it the Abbey Manor?), the canal cruisers in Bandit Country, Ajit and his fellow-Sikhs in Smethwick, Jorvan the Croat, the volunteer wardens in Netherton, even the unknown painter of SOCIAL VOMIT. Here's to them all.'

And I raised my glass of beer in a silent toast to all those who had helped to make our trip what it was - a journey to the warm, still-beating heart of the Black Country.

A BLACK COUNTRY BEAUTY SPOT

The loaded greenness held still in this canal
still holds the tonnage of working barges: recalls
them in the stroll-on progress of pleasure craft;
narrow boats, refurbished to cruise its unwinding.

I watch one now, entering Netherton Tunnel,
(The Long Tunnel, the Two Mile Tunnel, we kids
used to call it) past the info-board that discloses
its mystery at 2,768 metres;

even so, there are echoes of marvel. The thrumming
diesel, shoving into the South Portal, is disconnected
by the black in the name of the Black Country.
And though never inaudible will change accent

noticeably, through Rowley Hills to the north
of here, where Withymoor Island, Windmill End,
Hawne Basin and Bumble Hole would be uttered
from the finger-post with strangers' vowels.

I see this leant over the fresh painted balustrade
of one of three bridges back from the tunnel - a steadfast
geometry made whole in the water. This one is rutted;
its iron rope-scarred to tell me that horse-drawn

became man-hauled when bargees manoeuvred
packed barges - tugged the weight from this bridge -
into the spur. Passing a hand over these angled grooves
brings closer the technique of muscle and sweat;

the past of knack and finesse working to bend rules.
Raked and re-pointed, its chimney braced and made safe,
Cobb's Engine House stands and stands reflected
in the Cut too. It used to stymie the rise of water

in the pit that was here. Its stack chucking up
more black into our name. Now school kids model
it with a shoe box and toilet roll - marking its own spot
at the dead centre of how things were

is its new role. Worked-out becomes working out
as Slag-heap becomes View point over the Visitors' centre
with its sympathetic brick and old photos of the pit
and volunteers who share sandwiches with Canada geese.

They will explain the red island in Boshboil pool-
Furnace residue; a rusty wisp and whorl seeps
on to its surface like a whisper of the racket that forged
its name. Everything comes to the water, it says.

Me too, on my bridge with hard graft memories,
faced up in history and now to know something unended.

Stephen Clarke

Anyone seriously interested in the Black Country might find the following titles of interest - I certainly did!

Barnsby, George J [1980], *Social Conditions in the Black Country 1800 -1900*, Integrated Publishing Services

Bird, Vivian [1991], *The Priestley Riots 1791 and the Lunar Society*, Birmingham & Midland Institute

Burritt, Elihu [1976], *Walks in the Black Country and its Green Borderland*, The Roundwood Press

Chitham, Edward [1972], *The Black Country*, Longman

Davies, Ron [1987], *John Wilkinson*, Dulston Press

Dickinson, H.W. [1967], *James Watt: Craftsman and Engineer*, David & Charles

Dilworth, D [1973], *West Bromwich before the Industrial Revolution*, Black Country Society

Dodsworth, Roger [1996], *Glass and Glassmaking*, Shire Publications

Dudley MBC [1999], *A Strategy for Dudley's Canals*, Dudley MBC

Elwell, Charles [1991], *Aspects of the Black Country*, Black Country Society

Gibbons, Verna Hale [1998], *Jack Judge, the Tipperary Man*, Sandwell Community Library Service

Hackwood, F.W. [1895], *A History of West Bromwich*, Birmingham News & Printing Co.

Hadfield, Charles [1950], *British Canals*, David & Charles

Hill, Stan [1999], *Stan Hill's Brierley Hill and Life*, Black Country Society/Dulston Press

McGregor, Sheila [1999], *A Shared Vision: The Garman Ryan Collection at the New Art Gallery Walsall*, Merrell Holbertson

Nicholson/Ordnance Survey [1997], *Guide to the Waterways:Birmingham & the Heart of England*, Nicholson

Nicholson/Ordnance Survey [1997], *Guide to the Waterways:Severn, Avon & Birmingham*, Nicholson

Ordnance Survey [1995-97], *Landranger Map 139: Birmingham & Wolverhampton*, Ordnance Survey

Parsons, Harold [1986], *Portrait of the Black Country*, Robert Hale

Parsons, Harold [Ed.] [1968], *Black Country Stories*, Black Country Society

Pearson, Michael [1998], *Canal City Souvenir*, J.M.Pearson & Son

Pearson, Michael [1998], *Pearson's Canal Companion: Stourport Ring* J.M.Pearson & So

Raven, Jon & Totten, Malcolm [1975], *The Nailmakers*, Black Country Society

Raven, Jon [1978], *Tales from Aynuk's Black Country*, Broadside

Raven, Michael [1991, *Black Country Towns and Villages*, Broadside

Raybould, T.J. [1973], *The Economic Emergence of the Black Country*, David & Charles

Reeves, Frank [1989], *Race and Borough Politics*, Avebury

Richards, John [1993], *The History of Batham's Black Country Brewers*, Real Ale Books

Richardson, Eric [1996], *In Search of the Lost Canals of the Black Country*, Black Country Society

Truby, Arthur [1999], *Towpath Tale*, Ratchup Books

Tyzack, Don [1997], *Glass, Tools & Tyzacks*, Don Tyzack

Walker, Ted [1991], *The Black Country Trivia Quiz Book*, Ted Walker

Walker, Ted [undated], *The Definitive Black Country Dictionary*, Ted Walker

New In 2001

What For Chop Today?
Author: Gail Haddock

Editor: Joss Guttery

ISBN: 1903070074

RRP: £7.99

She joined VSO to save the world, save lives and save her soul.... finding a man and losing weight would be nice too, but you can't have everything.

Armed with these grand plans, a rucksack full of tampax and rubber gloves and a beginners guide to surgery, Gail Haddock swopped life as a York GP for non- stop action and adventure in a remote hospital of Sierra Leone.

Jasmine And Arnica - Nicola Naylor
Editor: Hazel Orme
ISBN: 1903070104
RRP: £7.99

An Indian Experience by the world's first blind travel writer.

Riding With Ghosts - South Of The Border -Gwen Maka
Editor: Gordon Medcalf
ISBN: 1903070090
RRP: £7.909

The second part of Gwen's epic cycle ride alone accross the American continent

Triumph Around The World - Robbie Marshall
Editor: Joss Guttery
ISBN: 1903070082
RRP: £7.99

For Robbie life really did start at 45 as he and his shiny new motorbike took to the open road.

Travellers Tales From Heaven And Hell - Part Three
Editor: Dan Hiscocks
ISBN: 1903070112
RRP: £6.99

More winners from our annual competition.

Cry From The Highest Mountain - Tess Burrows
Editor: Joss Guttery
ISBN:
RRP: £7.99

A struggle of body and mind in the fight to free a nation.

Jungle Janes

Author: Peter Burden

ISBN: 1903070058
RRP:£7.99

At a dinner party two bored army wives challenged their host Major Ken Hames that anything he could train men to do, they could do. In response he devised an expedition for 12 middle-aged women - A month long trek through the Primary Malaysian jungle.

We go beyond the battles with scorpions, snakes, spiders, giant hornets and further than the harrowing 12 hour treks to question whether the expedition was simply a battle of the sexes, or did it turn into something far more interesting?

Based on the documentary made by Anglia Television Ltd.

Travels With My Daughter

Author: Niema Ash

ISBN:190307004X
RRP:£7.99

"You could say I had an unconventional upbringing. At the age of four I was sharing my bedroom with Bob Dylan, and by the time I was fifteen I had been taken out of school to go travelling and was smoking joints with my mother".

This honest and often humorous account describes how Niema copes with:

>The desire to travel conflicting with the ties of motherhood.

>Finding the confidence to believe in herself and her instincts.

>Being a single mum in the sixties while mixing with some of the most talented poets and musicians of our time, including Bob Dylan,

>Leonard Cohen, Irving Layton, Seamus Heaney and Joni Mitchell.

>Developing a unique mother and daughter bond which many only dream about.

This book will touch a hidden nerve in everyone who reads it as it turns a world of convention and protocol upside-down!

Desert Governess

Author: Phyllis Ellis
Editor: Gordon Medcalf

ISBN: 1903070015
R.R.P: £7.99

In 1997 badly in need of a new start in life, Phyllis answered an advertisement: *English Governess wanted for Prince and Princesses of Saudi Arabian Royal Family.* She soon found herself whisked off to the desert to look after the children of HRH Prince Muqrin bin Abdul Aziz al Saud, the King's brother. In this frank personal memoir Phyllis describes her sometimes risky reactions to her secluded, alien lifestyle in a heavily guarded marble palace, allowed out only when chaperoned, veiled and clad from head to foot in black.

Both as a Governess and as a modern western woman she constantly ran up against frustrating prohibitions and unexpected moral codes, only a few of which she could work her way around – usually in the interests of her young royal charges.

Discovery Road

Authors: Tim Garratt & Andy Brown
Editor: Dan Hiscocks

ISBN: 0953057534
R.R.P: £7.99

Their mission and dream was to cycle around the southern hemisphere of the planet, with just two conditions. Firstly the journey must be completed within 12 months, and secondly, the cycling duo would have no support team or backup vehicle, just their determination, friendship and pedal power.

"Readers will surely find themselves reassessing their lives and be inspired to reach out and follow their own dreams."

Sir Ranulph Fiennes, Explorer

Fever Trees of Borneo
Author: Mark Eveleigh
Editor: Gordon Medcalf

ISBN: 095357569
R.R.P: £7.99

This is the story of how two Englishmen crossed the remotest heights of central Borneo, using trails no western eye had seen before, in search of the legendary 'Wild Men of Borneo'. On the way they encounter shipwreck, malaria, amoebic dysentery, near starvation, leeches, exhaustion, enforced alcohol abuse and barbecued mouse-deer foetus.

"Mark has the kind of itchy feet which will take more than a bucket of Johnson's baby talc to cure… he has not only stared death in the face, he has poked him in the ribs and insulted his mother."

Observer

Frigid Women
Authors: Sue & Victoria Riches
Editor: Gordon Medcalf

ISBN:0953057526
R.R.P:£7.99

In 1997 a group of twenty women set out to become the world's first all female expedition to the North Pole. Mother and daughter, Sue and Victoria Riches were amongst them. Follow the expedition's adventures in this true life epic of their struggle to reach one of Earth's most inhospitable places, suffering both physical and mental hardships in order to reach their goal, to make their dream come true.

"This story is a fantastic celebration of adventure, friendship, courage and love. Enjoy it all you would be adventurers and dream on."

Dawn French

Riding with Ghosts

Author: Gwen Maka

Editor: Gordon Medcalf

ISBN: 1903070007

R.R.P: £7.99

This is the frank, often outrageous account of a forty-something Englishwoman's epic 4,000 mile cycle ride from Seattle to Mexico, via the snow covered Rocky Mountains. She travels the length and breadth of the American West, mostly alone and camping in the wild. She runs appalling risks and copes in a gutsy, hilarious way with exhaustion, climatic extremes, dangerous animals, eccentrics, lechers and a permanently saddle-sore bum.

We share too her deep involvement with the West's pioneering past, and with the strong, often tragic traces history has left lingering on the land.

Slow Winter

Author: Alex Hickman

Editor: Gordon Medcalf

ISBN: 0953057585

R.R.P: £7.99

Haunted by his late father's thirst for adventure Alex persuaded his local paper that it needed a Balkan correspondent. Talking his way into besieged Sarajevo, he watched as the city's fragile cease fire fell apart. A series of chance encounters took him to Albania and a bizarre appointment to the government. Thrown into an alliance with the country's colourful dissident leader, he found himself occupying a ringside seat as corruption and scandal spilled the country into chaos.

This is a moving story of one man's search for his father's legacy among the mountains and ruin of Europe's oldest, and most mysterious corner.

The Jungle Beat – fighting terrorists in Malaya

Author: Roy Follows   ISBN: 0953057577
Editor: Dan Hiscocks   R.R.P: £7.99

This book describes, in his own words, the
experiences of a British officer in the Malayan Police
during the extended Emergency of the 1950's. It is the
story of a ruthless battle for survival against an
environment and an enemy which were equally deadly.
It ranks with the toughest and grimmest of the latter-
day SAS adventures.

*" It tells the story with no holds barred: war as war is. A compelling
reminder of deep jungle operations."*

General Sir Peter de la Billière

Touching Tibet

Author: Niema Ash   ISBN:0953057550
Editor: Dan Hiscocks   R.R.P:£7.99

After the Chinese invasion of 1950, Tibet remained
closed to travellers until 1984. When the borders were
briefly re-opened, Niema Ash was one of the few
people fortunate enough to visit the country before
the Chinese re-imposed their restrictions in 1987.
Touching Tibet is a vivid, compassionate, poignant
but often amusing account of a little known ancient
civilisation and a unique and threatened culture.

*"Excellent - Niema Ash really understands the situation facing Tibet and
conveys it with remarkable perception."*

Tenzin Choegyal (brother of The Dalai Lama)

Heaven & Hell

An eclectic collection of anecdotal travel stories – the best from thousands of entries to an annual competition. See website for details.

"…an inspirational experience. I couldn't wait to leave the country and encounter the next inevitable disaster." *The Independent*

Travellers' Tales from Heaven & Hell

Author: Various   ISBN: 0953057518
Editor: Dan Hiscocks   R.R.P: £6.99

More Travellers' Tales from Heaven & Hell

Author: Various   ISBN: 1903070023
Editor: Dan Hiscocks   R.R.P: £6.99

A Trail of Visions

Guide books tell you where to go, what to do and how to do it. A Trail of Visions shows and tells you how it feels.

"A Trail of Visions tells with clarity what it is like to follow a trail, both the places you see and the people you meet."

Independent on Sunday

"The illustrated guide."   The Times

Route 1: India, Sri Lanka, Thailand, Sumatra

Photographer / Author: Vicki Couchman
Editor: Dan Hiscocks ISBN: 1871349338
R.R.P: £14.99

Route 2: Peru, Bolivia, Ecuador, Columbia

Photographer / Author: Vicki Couchman
Editor: Dan Hiscocks ISBN: 093505750X
R.R.P: £16.99

TravellersEye Club Membership

Each month we receive hundreds of enquiries from people who've read our books or entered our competitions. All of these people have one thing in common: an aching to achieve something extraordinary, outside the bounds of our everyday lives. Not everyone can undertake the more extreme challenges, but we all value learning about other people's experiences.

Membership is free because we want to unite people of similar interests. Via our website, members will be able to liase with each other about everything from the kit they've taken, to the places they've been to and the things they've done. Our authors will also be available to answer any of your questions if you're planning a trip or if you simply have a question about their books.

As well as regularly up-dating members with news about our forthcoming titles, we will also offer you the following benefits:

Free entry to author talks / signings
Direct author correspondence
Discounts off new and past titles
Free entry to TravellersEye events
Discounts on a variety of travel products and services

To register your membership, simply write or email us telling us your name and address (postal and email). See address at the front of this book.

About TravellersEye

I believe the more you put into life, the more you get out of it. However, at times I have been disillusioned and felt like giving up on a goal because I have been made to feel that an ordinary person like me could never achieve my dreams.

The world is absolutely huge and out there for the taking. There has never been more opportunity for people like you and me to have dreams and fulfil them.

I have met many people who have achieved extraordinary things and these people have helped inspire and motivate me to try and live my life to the fullest.

TravellersEye publishes books about people who have done just this and we hope that their stories will encourage other people to live their dream.

When setting up TravellersEye I was given two pieces of advice. The first was that there are only two things I ever need to know: You are never going to know everything and neither is anyone else. The second was that there are only two things I ever need to do in life: Never give up and don't forget rule one.

Nelson Mandela said in his presidential acceptance speech: "Our deepest fear is not that we are inadequate. Our deepest fear is that we are powerful beyond our measure... as we let our own light shine, we unconsciously give other people permission to do the same."

We want people to shine their light and share it with others in the hope that it may encourage them to do the same.

Dan Hiscocks
Managing Director of TravellersEye